The draft Universal Credit Regulations 2013.

The Benefit Cap (Housing Benefit) Regulations 2012 (S.I. 2012 No. 2994)

The draft Universal Credit, Personal Independence Payment, Jobseeker's Allowance and Employment and Support Allowance (Claims and Payments) Regulations 2013.

Report by the Social Security Advisory Committee under Section 174(1) of the Social Security Administration Act 1992 and statement by the Secretary of State for Work and Pensions in accordance with Section 174(2) of that Act

Presented to Parliament by the Secretary of State for Work and Pensions pursuant to Section 174(2) of the Social Security Administration Act 1992.

December 2012 £21.50

ISBN: 9780108512155

Printed in the UK by The Stationery Office Limited
on behalf of the Controller of Her Majesty's Stationery Office

ID 2528584   12/12   25242   19585

Printed on paper containing 75% recycled fibre content minimum.

Contents

Statement by the Secretary of State for Work and Pensions in accordance with Section 174(2) of the Social Security Administration Act 1992.

The Universal Credit Regulations 2013.

The Benefit Cap (Housing Benefit) Regulations 2012.

The Universal Credit, Personal Independence Payment, Jobseeker's Allowance and Employment and Support Allowance (Claims and Payments) Regulations 2013.

Introduction

1.   The introduction of Universal Credit from October 2013 brings radical changes to the benefits system. It is a new, single system of means-tested support for working-age people in and out of work. Support for housing costs, children and childcare costs will be integrated and it will provide additions for disabled people and carers.

2.   On 8th March the Welfare Reform Act 2012 ("the Act"), which makes provision for the introduction of Universal Credit, received Royal Assent. The implementation of Universal Credit will require the passage of several sets of detailed regulations made under the provisions of the Act. The Universal Credit Regulations contain the detailed provisions to support the basic framework created by Part 1 of the Act. There are also a number of associated regulations making provisions for determining other aspects of Universal Credit such as making claims for and paying benefits, making decisions and providing for appeals against decisions. In addition, new regulations need to be made for Jobseeker's Allowance and Employment and Support Allowance so that they can function as contributory benefits alongside Universal Credit.

3.   The Social Security Advisory Committee (SSAC) considered several sets of these draft regulations and, between 15th June 2012 and 27th July 2012, conducted a consultation exercise with a broad range of organisations and individuals. In particular, the Committee examined the coherence of the package of regulations in terms of implementation, and whether there were gaps or unintended consequences that need to be addressed.

4.   There is no formal requirement to refer the principal Universal Credit regulations for consideration by the Committee[1]. Nevertheless, given the

---

[1] The draft Universal Credit Regulations and The Benefit Cap (Housing Benefit) Regulations were not subject to statutory referral to the Committee as it was planned that they be made within six months of the commencement of the relevant enabling power.

scope and importance of these reforms, Ministers asked SSAC to undertake a special exercise to scrutinise the regulations. The draft regulations were also published on the DWP website at:

http://www.dwp.gov.uk/policy/welfare-reform/legislation-and-key-documents/welfare-reform-act-2012/welfare-reform-draft-regulations/

5.   On 23rd August 2012, SSAC delivered its report on the Universal Credit and related regulations to the Secretary of State for Work and Pensions. The Committee's report is included in this document and follows the statement by the Secretary of State for Work and Pensions.

The Social Security Advisory Committee's Report

6.   SSAC undertook a public consultation exercise as part of their review and received just under 400 responses from individuals and organisations. The Committee reported that the majority of respondents were broadly supportive of the Government's ambitions to simplify the benefit system through the introduction of Universal Credit.

7.   The Committee's report, reflecting the majority of responses to the consultation, made 36 recommendations across six broad themes:

- Overarching issues;
- Self employment;
- Housing;
- The benefit cap;
- Conditionality and sanctions; and
- Claims and payments.

The report on Universal Credit and Conditionality

8.   The Committee has long taken an interest in conditionality and sanctions in the benefit system. In 2006 it undertook a review of the available evidence relating to sanctions within the UK benefits system and the wider international evidence relating to conditionality. Given the significant reforms to conditionality and sanctions heralded by the introduction of Universal Credit, the Committee reviewed, as an internal piece of work, the most recent research and provided an additional report on its findings to the Secretary of State with the intention of informing the implementation of the new approach to conditionality.

Government Response

9.   Universal Credit is the Government's key reform to tackle the two key problems of the current benefit system; poor work incentives and complexity. It will help people to move into and progress in work while supporting the most vulnerable. It will be simple to understand and administer and protect both the welfare of those most in need and the public purse. It will be a dynamic benefit, preparing the claimant for work wherever possible.

10.   The Secretary of State for Work and Pensions welcomes the Committee's report on the Universal Credit and related regulations which was completed to a challenging timescale. The Secretary of State welcomes the constructive and practical set of recommendations and is also grateful to the Committee and its Secretariat for providing separate technical and drafting comments on

the Regulations. DWP officials have responded in full to the Committee's technical comments and this will be published by the Committee on its website at:

http://ssac.independent.gov.uk/

11. The Secretary of State welcomes the acknowledgement that proposals for simplifying the benefit system have the broad support of a significant number of consultation respondents. He also welcomes the focus on both the practical aspects of delivery and its consideration of the overall coherence of the package of regulations. The Secretary of State also agrees with the Committee that the Department for Work and Pensions should monitor and evaluate the impact of the implementation of Universal Credit.

Piloting Powers

12. Implementing a system that is dynamic and responsive is at the heart of these reforms. This is why the Act contains a provision in Section 41 (Pilot Schemes) to enable the piloting of changes to the system that aim to achieve simplification or change claimant behaviour to improve their labour market outcomes. The Secretary of State recognises the importance of transparency. Therefore regulations to support any pilot scheme will be subject to the affirmative resolution procedure and will be time-limited.

Conclusion

13. Overall, the Secretary of State is pleased to accept most of the Committee's 36 recommendations which are addressed in the following six sections.

Overarching issues

Committee recommendations

14. The Committee identified a number of overarching issues common to the regulations upon which it consulted. The Committee recommended that both regulations and underpinning guidance should contain clear definitions in order that benefit decisions so derived be equally clear and unambiguous.

15. The Committee acknowledged the radical approach taken to welfare reform through Universal Credit and noted that it would be crucial to the credibility of the Government's reforms that adequate monitoring and evaluation be put in place to allow rapid and informed responses to emerging issues.

16. In noting the scale of the IT programme necessary to support the implementation of Universal Credit, the Committee suggested considering carefully the impact of any amendments to regulations on IT delivery plans, continuing to hold discussions, at a senior level, with other Government departments and to consider carefully the classification of Universal Credit as a social assistance benefit.

Government response

17. The Government acknowledges the helpful suggestions made by the Committee on a number of overarching issues important to the general development and implementation of Universal Credit. In general, the Government agrees with the Committee's recommendations.

18. **The Government agrees with the Committee that regulations and underpinning guidance should contain clear and unambiguous definitions.**

19. **The Government also agrees with the Committee on the importance of evaluating and monitoring the effects of Universal Credit.** Universal Credit marks a fundamental change to the way in which people engage with the benefit system and access in-work financial support. Its design, implementation and delivery will span a number of years. Evaluation plans will reflect both the long timescale and complexity of the reform. That means that a wide-ranging evaluation strategy will be developed which employs a number of different approaches over the lifetime of the policy. These will range from ongoing monitoring, 'live running reviews' of implementation and delivery through to longer term analysis of the outcomes and impacts for different groups of claimants from implementation through to 2017 and beyond.

20. The Committee recommended that the Government consider carefully the impact of amendments to the regulations on the delivery of the IT supporting Universal Credit. **The Government agrees that it is critical to consider the technical implications of regulatory amendments**. However, it is also important to understand that the Department is developing the Universal Credit IT in a new and radical way. IT is being developed in incremental 'builds' based on sequential release cycles. Before being accepted for inclusion in the release schedule, all proposals for regulatory amendments were evaluated for their impact on the IT design and build. As a result, the Department is on track to take account of regulatory adjustments and still deliver the national rollout of Universal Credit from October 2013.

21. The Committee suggested that the Department might wish to consider further the classification of Universal Credit in the context of EU legislation on social security coordination (Regulations 883/2004 and 1408/71). **The Department has considered Universal Credit in relation to these and other EU regulations**. In particular, it has considered Regulation 492/11, on the basis that Universal Credit is a new single benefit rather than on the basis that it is an agglomeration of existing benefits which, indeed, are treated differently in the EU context. The way in which Universal Credit provides support to people in particular circumstances is different from the way that existing benefits do, and, as the Committee recognises, it is not a straightforward task to assess all the implications of EU legislation. The Department has concluded that Universal Credit is outside the scope of EU Regulation 883/04 and, as such, is not exportable. It is within the scope of other EU legislation and will be treated accordingly.

Self-employment

Committee recommendations

22. The Committee noted the Government's commitment to encouraging self-employment, reducing the burdens on business whilst supporting benefit take-up. Nevertheless, whilst welcoming the simplifications introduced through Universal Credit, the Committee recommended that the Government recognise that the range of people, capabilities and working patterns of self-employed people is as broad and diverse as the overall labour market and to continue to engage with industry groups in order to understand and minimise the impacts on business.

23. The Committee also recommended that the Government give clear guidance on the status, in terms of conditionality and more generally, of quasi self-employed claimants and those not actively developing a business. It also recommended that a degree of flexibility be permitted as the policy in relation to self-employment is implemented.

24. The Committee recommended that the Government consider ways in which the reporting of self-employed earnings might help to reduce administrative burdens, costs and complexity experienced by business. In particular, the Committee recommended that the Government give further consideration to its policies on monthly reporting of earnings and alignment with wider government self-employment rules, permitted expenses and rolling forward losses and for allowing more than one start-up period in a lifetime. It also recommended that the Government consider a full reconciliation of self-employed business gains and losses balanced with Self Assessment returns and, together with HM Revenue and Customs, to move towards a unified reporting regime.

Government response

25. The Government recognises that self-employment provides a vital contribution to the economy and it will be an important contributor to the sustained recovery from recession. Universal Credit is therefore being designed so that it provides the right support for self-employed people on lower incomes.

26. As part of its wider growth strategy, the Government is keen to help self-employed people to achieve their potential and to progress in work. A balance, though, must be achieved. Universal Credit should support people to be self-employed, but only insofar as self-employment is the best route for them to become financially self-sufficient.

27. To ensure the policy meets these aims, **the Government agrees with the Committee and has been keen to use the consultation on the Welfare Reform regulations to engage industry stakeholders.** This engagement provided an excellent opportunity for stakeholders to scrutinise, and provide comment on, the self-employment policy and regulations. This led to further engagement between stakeholders and policy officials. Meetings have been held with a number of groups including:

- Prince's Trust;
- AAT: the professional body for accounting technicians;
- Low Income Tax Reform Group;
- Chartered Institute of Taxation;
- Administrative Burdens Advisory Board; and
- Institute of Chartered Accountants for England and Wales

28. In addition, The Minister for Welfare Reform has undertaken a series of meetings with stakeholders.

29. Discussions with these groups have greatly helped stakeholders to understand the policy and have alleviated some of the stakeholder concerns.

30. **The Government agrees with the emphasis the Committee has placed on the importance of correctly identifying those who are technically 'self-employed' but would be more appropriately treated as an individual seeking employed work, and those who are self-employed and developing their business.**

31. Vital to the success of Universal Credit is ensuring that claimants start their journey on the right pathway based on their individual circumstances. Where a claimant declares that they are self-employed, an initial gateway interview will examine if they have a genuine business or business proposition with actual or realistic expectations of profit. If so, they may therefore be determined as gainfully self-employed rather than in fact an employee or someone who should be seeking employed work.

32. Stakeholders were concerned that DWP did not have the expertise to undertake this task. To address this, officials asked for stakeholder input into the supporting adviser guidance which advisers will use at the gateway interview. The first stakeholder session was held on 15th October 2012 and was received positively by those who attended.

33. The Government also recognises the need for claimants who are setting up a business to be given time to establish themselves and develop their business and customer base. Therefore, where a claimant has been self-employed for less than 12 months a start up period will be granted. This means that claimants will not be required to satisfy work-search or availability

requirements, and the Minimum Income Floor will not be applied thereby giving them time to concentrate on developing their business.

34. **The Government has studied the Committee's recommendations, and listened to the representations of others such as the Low Income Tax Reform Group and the Chartered Institute of Taxation on the issue**. As a result, the Government has decided to allow further start up periods for self-employed claimants; one new start up period every 5 years. This strikes the right balance between supporting new business and protecting the public purse by ensuring that people do not abuse the system.

35. In order to calculate a claimant's Universal Credit award accurately, the DWP need to know what someone is earning each month. Monthly reporting allows Universal Credit to be adjusted on a monthly basis, which will ensure that claimants whose income from self-employment falls do not have to wait several months for a rise in their Universal Credit.

36. For self-employed claimants this means we require them to report their earnings as close to the end of the assessment period as possible, preferably within seven calendar days, in order to ensure prompt receipt of their Universal Credit award. If the claimant does not report their income by that date, they have a further week to report at which point, if earnings information has still not been received, they will receive a notification informing them that they have a further month to report. If nothing is received by then the award of Universal Credit will be terminated.

37. The Government has also listened to stakeholders' concerns on the current inability to carry forward losses from previous assessment periods under Universal Credit and **agrees with the Committee's recommendations to revisit this issue**. As a result, DWP are considering the feasibility of a carry forward function in the future.

38. The Government has been clear that, where possible, income reporting for self-employed claimants will be aligned with the new cash income reporting system that HMRC are developing to simplify tax. To ensure this happens, DWP and HMRC are working closely together on the two systems to make them as simple as possible. The Government has an ambition that the information collected for the monthly submissions required for Universal Credit can be used for tax purposes at the end of the year. Inevitably there will be some differences as the two systems are designed to do different things; however both departments are committed to aligning the systems where possible.

39. **The Government agrees with the Committee that the impact of reforms on self-employed people should be monitored, particularly in terms of the interactions with the monthly assessment of Universal Credit.** So the evaluation strategy will employ a number of different approaches such as

ongoing monitoring and 'live running reviews' of implementation in order to learn lessons and reflect them in future delivery.

40. **The Government does not agree that it will be necessary to pilot these new arrangements now but retains the power in Section 41 of the Act to consider different approaches in the future should it prove to be necessary.** Indeed, the trialing of different approaches may be more effective when a sufficient number of self-employed claimants have begun to receive Universal Credit. The implementation of Universal Credit will also be subject to comprehensive monitoring arrangements.

Housing

Committee recommendations

41. The Committee acknowledged the principle underlying Universal Credit that individual claimants should take more responsibility for their own financial affairs. This principle is enshrined in the way in which housing support is provided for in Universal Credit.

42. The Committee made a number of recommendations in respect of housing support. In general, the Committee recommended that the Government should consider the practical aspects of implementation as well as understanding, and mitigating, unintended consequences on vulnerable people. In particular, the Committee recommended that the Government consider the consequences of the policy on vulnerable people in the following policy areas:

    - The direct payment of housing support;
    - The monthly payment of Universal Credit particularly in relation to claimants fleeing domestic violence;
    - Service charges;
    - The under-occupation of social-rented sector accommodation; and
    - The 'zero earnings rule' in mortgage support.

43. The Committee acknowledged that the policy on supported housing was still undergoing active development and recommended that the Government consider consultation responses, such as taking supported accommodation out of Universal Credit, when developing its plans.

Government response

44. Universal Credit will include an amount to help meet eligible housing costs. The policy intent is to broadly replicate the eligibility rules for liabilities covered by the current Housing Benefit and support for mortgage interest schemes. In line with the commitments in the White Paper, arrangements will provide for simplification and consistency with the general aims of Universal Credit.

Under-occupation

45. **The Government has considered the case for specific exemptions to the under-occupation measure in the social-rented sector but does not believe that such an approach would be an effective use of scarce resources.** The Government believes that exemptions tend to be broad brush and do not sufficiently target help on those most in need. Instead of exemptions, an additional £30 million a year has been provided for the

Discretionary Housing Payment fund over the Spending Review period aimed primarily at assisting those in significantly adapted properties and foster carers. Local authority staff are better able to identify genuine need and to judge what is appropriate on an individual, case-by-case basis. Nevertheless, the Government will monitor the impacts of this measure carefully to inform the ongoing delivery of housing cost support within Universal Credit.

46. It should be noted that, while there is not a separate run-on for housing costs in Universal Credit, the recently bereaved are entitled to a run-on of the whole of their benefit for a period of 3 months. Under the current system most income replacement benefits are reduced immediately on the death of a family member. The Universal Credit rules will also provide that, where someone normally resident in the property is temporarily absent, there is usually no adjustment to size criteria for a period of 6 months. The period may be shorter in cases where the absent person in abroad. An additional room is allowed where an adult needs overnight care.

Supported Exempt Accommodation and Refuges

47. **Having considered the Committee's recommendations, as well as listening to the views of stakeholders, the Government has decided that help towards housing costs for those living in supported exempt accommodation[2] will be provided outside of Universal Credit.** This means that organisations such as homeless hostels and women's refuges that come within the ambit of this provision will continue to receive help on a similar basis to now. This will remove the difficulties associated with monthly awards in Universal Credit and provide a flexible system to help meet the higher costs often associated with providing this type of accommodation.

48. In the short term this help will be delivered broadly as now through local authorities under existing DWP legislation and funding arrangements. This means that people living in supported accommodation will still be able to claim and receive Universal Credit to meet other living costs but help with their housing costs will be provided for separately. For the longer term the Department is exploring the feasibility of a localised funding system. This is because local knowledge is essential to help identify this often diverse group, build effective relationships with providers and ensure that resources are targeted effectively at those who need it.

---

[2] This refers to a specific type of accommodation defined as 'exempt' supported accommodation as currently set out in DWP legislation. That is either: a resettlement place; or accommodation provided by a county council, housing association registered charity or voluntary organisation where that body or person acting on their behalf provides the claimant with care, support or supervision.

Legislative reference: Paragraphs 4 and 5 of schedule 3 to the Housing Benefit and Council Tax Benefit (Consequential Provisions) Regulations 2006 (SI 2006 No. 217)

49. The Government is not looking to reduce expenditure in this area but the system will, as now, investigate where costs appear unreasonably high. Local knowledge plays a big part in determining whether costs are reasonable and a locally administered system will ensure that any scrutiny results in a fair assessment. This approach will ease concerns over funding and payment regimes particularly for refuges and hostels that come within the ambit of the provision. At the same time it will allow flexibility in developing future funding systems.

Direct payments

50. **The Government agrees with the Committee that more people should be encouraged to handle their own financial affairs themselves.** The Government also takes seriously the legitimate concerns of landlords, whether operating in the social or private-rented sectors, over the security of income. This is why trials are ongoing to demonstrate the processes that will support claimants managing their own rent and benefit payments as well as the mechanism to enable payments to be switched to the landlord when they cannot. These demonstration projects are subject to full monitoring and evaluation.

51. More information is provided at paragraph 98 below.

Service charges

52. Housing cost provisions within Universal Credit will include help for eligible service charges that the tenant or home owner is liable to pay. As now, no provision will be made to support ineligible service charges such as meals, personal care or personal utility bills where it would be wrong to make provision or support is provided from elsewhere in the welfare system.

53. The Government will not be making significant changes in respect of the charges that are eligible or ineligible. The difference between the approach in Universal Credit compared to Housing Benefit and is that Universal Credit guidance will start from a principle of eligibility. Guidance for landlords will state explicitly which services charges are eligible. This approach is designed to be simpler and less time-consuming than the current approach in Housing Benefit.

54. **The Government agrees with the Committee's recommendation on service charges.** DWP has been consulting widely to inform the service charges guidance. A number of landlords, landlord groups and housing professionals (including the NHF, COSLA and CH Cymru) have been involved in helping to develop the guidance. The Department sought input from the Scottish and Welsh Governments, as well as the Valuation Office Agency (and their Scottish and Welsh counterparts) and the Department for Communities

and Local Government. A wider consultation will be conducted ahead of publication of the guidance.

Zero earnings rule for mortgage support

55.   Mortgage support in Universal Credit will broadly replicate current provisions in Jobseeker's Allowance, Employment and Support Allowance and Income Support. There will, however, be a 'zero earnings rule' which means that there will be no eligibility for help with housing costs if the claimant or their partner is doing any paid work. Currently there is no help with mortgage payments in tax credits but a small number of people do work part time and continue to receive help with their mortgages in the income-related benefits.

56.   The Government believes that most owner occupiers should be aiming to move from short-term help with their housing costs into full-time work. The Government should not underwrite a decision to engage in part-time work if this does not enable an individual to service their mortgage. Owner-occupiers who do only small amounts of work will need to re-consider their position with regard to the amount of work they do or the level of their housing costs.

57.   However, we recognise that there are circumstances where part-time work may be appropriate. For example, for those using part-time employment as a stepping stone back to the labour market. In many cases these people will be better off under Universal Credit even though the housing costs element will cease. This is because there is a small earnings disregard only in the current system, with income above that level taken into account pound for pound. The more generous earnings disregard in Universal Credit will mean that only those doing a very small amount of work are likely to be worse off than now.

58.   To illustrate the impact of the zero earnings rule, take the example of a lone parent who decides to take advantage of the offer of 15 hours a week free nursery education and moves into part-time work. She is receiving the average amount of mortgage support (£37 a week) and is paid at the national minimum wage. Under Universal Credit, she will need to work just seven hours a week to be better off in work, despite the withdrawal of her mortgage support. If she works for 10 hours or more a week she will be better off than she would be under the current system. Clearly, if her hourly rate is higher than the national minimum her income will rise more quickly as she increases her hours.

The benefit cap

Committee recommendations

59.   The Government intends, subject to certain exceptions, to limit the amount of benefit that an out-of-work household of working age can receive. The Committee has already made recommendations intended to alleviate the impact of the policy on certain groups which the Government has been pleased to accept. The Committee acknowledges the Government's strategy to inform claimants early that their benefit may be affected. Nevertheless, the Committee recommends that the Government and local authorities monitor and evaluate the wider effect of the policy carefully and make adjustments to the policy where necessary.

Government response

60.   The Government believes that a person in work should be better off than a person on benefits and that it is not fair that people can receive more on out-of-work benefits than the earnings of the average working family in Great Britain. Therefore, a cap on benefits will be introduced from April 2013 and will apply to the combined income from the main out-of-work benefits, plus Housing Benefit, Child Benefit and Child Tax Credit.

61.   The purpose behind the cap is to encourage people to change their circumstances, and above all to work. Therefore households entitled to Working Tax Credit and, under Universal Credit, households with earnings of £430 a month or more will be exempt.

62.   The level of the benefit cap will be set with reference to average earnings (after tax and National Insurance) for working families. On the introduction of Universal Credit, the cap will be set at £2167 per month for couple and single parent households and £1517 per month for single adult households.

63.   Households in receipt of: War widows or widowers pension; the support component of Employment and Support Allowance; Disability Living Allowance (and its successor Personal Independence Payment) or Attendance Allowance; Industrial Injuries Benefits; War Disablement Pension and equivalent payments under the Armed Forces Compensation Scheme; or the Limited Capability for Work and Work Related Activity element of Universal Credit will be exempt.

64.   Payments towards childcare costs will be ignored when applying the benefit cap.

65.   **The Government has considered the Committee's recommendations and is ensuring that ongoing engagement takes place with individual**

organisations that have a key interest on how the benefit cap will impact on their particular client group. Officials are working closely with representatives from Local Government Associations, Homeless Link, Shelter and Refuge, to identify the particular issues and develop solutions to provide the support required for claimants both before and during the transitional phase of the cap's implementation in April 2013.

66. **The Government has also promised, in agreement with the Committee's recommendation, to publish a review of the cap in 2014 following its first year of operation.** The review will attempt to evaluate the effect of the cap on the number of people who are currently receiving more than the threshold and thus will have their benefit payment reduced in April 2013. The aim is to provide as full picture as possible to this timescale and this will include, as far as feasible, early indications of impact on encouraging people to move off benefit; on where claimants can afford to live; and, if practicable, the initial impacts on vulnerable individuals. It will also assess savings against those forecast in the impact assessment. The review will feed into the Department's longer term plans for evaluation of the cap.

Conditionality and sanctions

Committee recommendations

67. The Committee recognised the importance of effective sanctions to the proper operation of the benefit system and received a number of responses on the subject. Furthermore, it recognised the clear link between sanctions and the Claimant Commitment; the agreement between the Government and the claimant to provide welfare support in return for work related activity appropriate to the claimant and their circumstances. The Committee recommended that the Claimant Commitment be more of a personalised contract between the Government and the individual so that it meets the legitimate needs of both parties. It also recommended that sanctions should be suspended when the claimant re-engages with the commitment to which they have agreed. The Committee also recommended that in-work conditionality be regulated for separately from out-of-work conditionality to recognise the differences in approach between the two. The Committee also endorsed the need for robust and comprehensive evaluation of the new sanction arrangements.

68. In addition to the main report, the Committee reviewed recent research and produced a separate report on conditionality and sanctions. The Committee invited the Secretary of State to consider this report alongside their wider report on Universal Credit.

Government response

69. To be entitled to Universal Credit claimants must accept a Claimant Commitment. For those expected to search for work, a personalised Claimant Commitment will be drawn up by their personal adviser during a face-to-face discussion.

70. **The Government agrees with the Committee that the Claimant Commitment should be personalised** and requirements should be tailored to the individual claimant's circumstances and capability. Detailed guidance will support this. The Claimant Commitment will be revised on an on-going basis to record clearly the expectations placed upon a claimant, based on what can be reasonably expected of them given their capability and circumstances, and the consequences (sanctions) of any failure to comply.

71. If a claimant refuses to accept their Claimant Commitment then they will not be entitled to Universal Credit. As Universal Credit is a household benefit, if either eligible adult in a couple refuses to accept their Claimant Commitment then the claim for the other eligible adult will also end. Where a claimant does refuse to accept their Claimant Commitment we will allow a short 'cooling off' period to give the claimant the opportunity to reconsider their decision and the impact on the household claim.

72. But in exceptional circumstances, where a claimant is unable to accept a Claimant Commitment, we intend to remove the requirement to do so. This may include, for example, certain claimants who have an appointee or someone acting on their behalf; claimants who are incapacitated in hospital and where exceptional emergency situations exist. Also, for claimants with no or limited work related requirements, it is expected that the initial Claimant Commitment will be accepted as part of the normal claims process.

73. The Government expects Universal Credit claimants to do all they reasonably can to establish an adequate level of earnings. However, when they are unable to meet any work related requirements because of particular circumstances and capability, or because they already have an adequate level of earnings, they will fall outside the Universal Credit labour market regime and into the No Work Related Requirements group. The regulations will set out clearly who is and is not subject to conditionality. However, the Government agrees with the Committee and consequently is taking a staged approach to the introduction of in-work conditionality.

74. On in-work conditionality, the Government wants to introduce interventions that help employed claimants who are earning under their conditionality earnings threshold to move into more work or better paid work. The regime that will be put in place for this in-work group is still under development and DWP Ministers have been clear that before applying in-work conditionality a series of different interventions will be piloted that will build evidence and understanding of this group.

75. Details of the initial in-work conditionality regime will be set out in adviser guidance and other related products and will therefore not require additional regulations.

76. The Welfare Reform Act sets out that sanctions will be imposed on Universal Credit claimants who fail to meet conditionality requirements without a good reason. The sanctions regime will drive engagement with conditionality requirements by providing clarity for claimants about the consequences of non-compliance; providing a robust deterrent against non-compliance; and tougher sanctions for repeated non-compliance.

77. Sanctions will apply at one of four different levels. Lowest level sanctions will be applied to claimants subject to work-focused interview requirements only who fail to participate in a work-focused interview or connected requirement without good reason. Low level sanctions will be applied where a claimant fails without good reason to comply with a requirement designed to help them move into or to prepare for work. Medium level sanctions will be imposed when a claimant fails without good reason to undertake all reasonable work search action or be able and willing immediately to take up work. High level sanctions will be imposed where a claimant fails, without good reason, to meet the most important requirements relating to employment opportunities.

78. The sanctions regime will incorporate a range of safeguards for claimants. In particular, requirements placed on claimants will be reasonable, taking into account their capability and circumstances, for example because of health conditions, disability and caring responsibilities. Sanctions will not be applied if a claimant can show good reason for non-compliance with a requirement. And where a claimant is in receipt of the maximum amount, sanctions will not affect the Universal Credit amounts available for housing, children and disability.

79. The Government believes that, in order to support people into work, there should be meaningful sanctions for failure to comply with reasonable conditionality requirements. The Committee has suggested that the Government should undertake robust and comprehensive evaluation of the new sanction arrangements and **the Government is pleased to accept this recommendation.** As part of the formal programme to evaluate Universal Credit, in-depth qualitative work with staff and claimants is planned. This will include questions on sanctions, sanctioning processes and claimant reactions to having been sanctioned. An expert group, including both internal and external advisers, has been convened to inform the development of the evaluation.

80. The Committee also recommended that a sanction should be suspended when a claimant re-engages with their conditionality requirements. In fact, low level sanctions will have an open-ended element that come to end when the claimant complies with a specific requirement. However, **the Government does not agree that the concept of re-engagement can be applied to failures such as leaving employment voluntarily or failing to complete work-search activity** but has made provisions that will terminate sanctions where the claimant has been earning at the level expected of them for 26 weeks. In addition, the application and effectiveness of sanctions will be monitored closely and a power, at Section 41 of the Act, exists to pilot different approaches in the future.

The report on Universal Credit and conditionality

81. As stated at paragraph 8 above, the Secretary of State is grateful for the Committee's separate report on Universal Credit and conditionality. The Government does differ on some of the conclusions reached in the report, for example it would place greater emphasis on the deterrent effect of sanctions, but there is a great deal of agreement between the Government and the Committee on the key issues raised in the report. In particular:

- The Government agrees substantially with the report's main conclusions that claimants should be clear about the requirements placed upon them and about the sanctions they will face. The Department will be working to ensure that the design of the Claimant Commitment supports this objective.

- The Government agrees that advisers and decision makers should take the claimant's circumstances into account when setting requirements and considering whether to apply a sanction.

- The Government agrees that effective relationships between advisers, claimants and partners are important in underpinning the conditionality and sanctions regime.

82. Overall, the Government welcomes this helpful report. It agrees that fairness, re-engagement and safeguards should be features of a sanctions regime and looks forward to working with the Committee as Guidance and communication products are developed to support such an approach.

Claims and payments

Committee recommendations

83. The Government intends that Universal Credit be delivered, by default, using digital channels and the Committee recognised the advantages of effective on-line systems, both for government and for individuals. It recommended that the Government put in place the necessary resources, such as information, to support claimants initially unable to make their claims on-line and to make access to on-line channels as straightforward as possible.

84. The Committee welcomed the move towards monthly payment but noted the potential for disruption to the budgeting of people more used to weekly or fortnightly payment of benefits. The Committee looked forward to receiving detailed proposals around providing educational resources on financial management and learning the findings of the Demonstration Projects; projects aimed to demonstrate the support systems and switching mechanisms underpinning the payment of housing costs in Universal Credit. The Committee also recommended that, in certain circumstances, the Government retain 'good cause' provision for the backdating of a Universal Credit claim.

85. The Committee noted the Government's intention to require couples to make a joint claim to Universal Credit but recommended that clear guidance be produced and that, in some cases, one member of the couple could be paid as a single person to avoid hardship. The Committee also recommended that personal information, especially address information, be protected when couples separate due to domestic violence.

Government response

Digital by default

86. The Government's intention is that Universal Credit will be digital by default, putting claimants at the heart of the service and giving them greater control over managing their account. The claims process will be as simple as possible for both claimants and administrators and has been designed to provide a predominantly online, self-service benefit where the claimant is able to manage their Universal Credit account online.

87. Universal Credit provides a real opportunity to tackle digital exclusion. People with poor or no digital skills are excluded from 92 per cent of advertised vacancies that require applicants to have basic IT skills, are likely to earn 10 per cent less and miss out on job vacancies from the 25 per cent of employers who advertise online only. By encouraging and supporting claimants to manage their accounts online, their digital capability is being enhanced, helping them to get back into work.

88. The Government is designing the service carefully working with claimants to design a service driven by users. It is also working across Departments to help those without internet access get on-line and working with digital champions.

89. **As recommended by the Committee, the Government is working on Knowledge Management systems to ensure that guidance notes and information documents are clear and unambiguous so that users understand how to access services.**

90. Alternative channels will also be available for vulnerable people and all claimants will have access to the full range of support, dependent on need and irrespective of location. In exceptional cases, face to face contact will be offered for people who are unable to use either the online or telephony channels. Initially, this is likely to involve the claimant visiting a local office or receiving a home visit from the delivery organisation, where a digital form can be completed. The Department has been working with HMRC and local authority representatives to produce a collaborative design.

91. **The Government agrees with the Committee that effective communications are required for those claimants who are less able to maintain their Universal Credit account.** The Department is working on providing alternative access provisions including allowing claimants to access their accounts from a smart phone web browser leading eventually to a Universal Credit application for smart phones later in the rollout.

92. The Government expects that the vast majority of claimants will use the digital service by 2017. In line with the Committee's recommendation, we anticipate a gradual increase in take up between October 2013 and 2017. The Government continues to explore how best to provide digital skills support for those who need it.

93. **The Government also agrees with the Committee that financial management education is important to help some claimants manage their finances more effectively.** The Department is working with the advice sector to determine the types of money advice services needed to help claimants as they move to Universal Credit. Examples of the types of advice under consideration include: advice on managing money and paying bills including how to do a monthly budget plan; motivating and increasing confidence to take control of personal finances; prioritising and paying rent on time; and advice on how to set up and manage bank accounts.

Monthly payment

94. Universal Credit will be paid in arrears on a calendar monthly basis in a single payment. The monthly assessment period will run from the effective date of claim and each subsequent assessment period will begin on the same date

each month. A claimant's initial Universal Credit pay date will be seven calendar days after the end of their initial monthly assessment period to allow for four BACS processing days plus any non-working days such as weekends and bank holidays. To help existing claimants move from fortnightly legacy benefit payments to a monthly award of Universal Credit, a fair, simple and affordable means will be provided to ensure that they do not experience a significant shortfall in cash flow in the first month. Claimants migrating onto Universal Credit will therefore be provided with the option of an advance of payment two weeks into their first Universal Credit assessment period.

95. This broad approach reflects the world of work where the majority of people receive wages monthly. Paying in this manner will help smooth the transition into monthly paid work, encourage personal responsibility for finances and support claimants to budget on a monthly basis.

96. **Alongside the Committee, the Government recognises that some claimants may need additional help to budget, particularly during the transitional period.** The Department is working with the advice sector to ensure that claimants are able to access appropriate budgeting support services to enable them to manage their money successfully. Work is also being undertaken to make a supplier assessment of existing and future budgeting advice services with a view to determining the potential provision and any shortfall against demand.

97. **The Government is also considering the Committee's recommendation on the timing of Universal Credit payments, for example to coincide with pre-existing direct debit payments and will evaluate the impact of the policy during implementation.**

Direct payments

98. The Government wants to ensure that the experience of those Universal Credit claimants who are out of work mirrors, as far as possible, that of other families who are in work. This is in order to make the move into work and eventually off benefits, where appropriate, as smooth as possible. For that reason, the Government's starting position is that people should manage their own budgets in the same way as households in work. Therefore, the approach in Universal Credit will be to move away from making payments direct to third parties including landlords.

99. **The Government shares the views of the Committee in that alternative payment arrangements may be needed for some claimants to support them in the move to Universal Credit.** This could be a more frequent payment, a split payment within the household or payment of housing costs direct to the landlord.

100.	The direct payment Demonstration Projects are also providing an opportunity to test support and exceptions proposals. The Government has commissioned a review of the projects led by Professor Paul Hickman from the Centre for Regional Economic and Social Research at Sheffield Hallam University. The review will evaluate the impact of direct payments on claimants and vulnerable groups, as well as local authorities and social rented sector landlords. As recommended by the Committee, the findings will be able to influence the ongoing delivery of Universal Credit.

101.	The projects are running from June 2012 until June 2013 with approximately 2,000 tenants involved in each of the six local authority areas. Working with social-sector landlords, they are trialling how tenants can manage monthly payments ahead of the introduction of Universal Credit. Expert workshops are also being held to help inform the development of financial support. Issues of individual and household finances are being looked at in the evaluation.

Joint claims

102.	Where a couple claim Universal Credit, and one of the members does not meet one or more of the basic conditions of entitlement, then differing rules may apply depending on the condition that is not met. Specific situations, where different rules may need to apply, have been identified. These are where only one member of the couple satisfies Universal Credit eligibility criteria; where a couple are erroneously claiming as two single claimants; and where one member of a couple refuses to accept their individual Claimant Commitment.

103.	When two people claim Universal Credit as a couple but only one of the couple fulfils certain other basic conditions of entitlement, the claim will be treated as being a single claim from the claimant who fulfils the conditions of entitlement. However, any income and capital belonging to the ineligible claimant will also be treated as belonging to the claimant who is eligible.

104.	Where two people claim Universal Credit as single claimants and, as a result of information provided by the claimants or through further enquiry, it is determined that they are a couple, the separate claims may be treated as a joint claim. If it is determined that the couple have contrived to present themselves as single people in order to maximise their overall Universal Credit award, their separate claims will be disallowed.

105.	In order for both members of a couple making a claim to Universal Credit to be entitled to the benefit they must each accept their individual Claimant Commitment. If one member of the couple does not accept their claimant commitment, neither will be eligible if they continue to apply as a couple. A 'cooling off' period will be allowed for claimants to re-consider accepting their Claimant Commitment before any decision is taken.

106. The Government has considered the Committee's recommendation that, where one member of a couple fails to make a Claimant Commitment, the other member of the couple could be paid as a single person to avoid hardship. **The Government believes, however, that this would undermine the principle that the working age members of households claiming Universal Credit should agree, and be held to, reasonable commitments to engage in looking for work and taking up work.** Nevertheless, where a claimant has separated from their partner following a failed joint claim because the ex-partner refused to agree their Claimant Commitment, they may then make a claim as a single person. In these circumstances their single claim will be backdated to the date of their previous joint claim, subject to a maximum period of one month. The Government will monitor the impact of these arrangements.

107. The Committee also asked that the Government put in place procedures to safeguard confidential information, particularly address information, when couples separate due to domestic violence. **The Government agrees with this recommendation and is putting in place arrangements to ensure that, in these cases, confidential information will not be visible to either party online.**

Backdating

108. The date of claim for a Universal Credit claimant will be the date that a claim is submitted via the online service or the date on which a claim made by telephone is properly completed. It is also a basic condition of entitlement that all claimants must agree a Claimant Commitment.

109. For those claims not made online by the claimant personally – where for instance a claimant requires a home visit, or a face-to-face appointment, or where a telephone claim cannot be taken on the date that the person wishes – the date of that first contact should be treated as the effective date of claim.

110. The Committee recommended that the Government retain 'good cause' backdating provisions such as where a claimant has received misleading benefit advice. **The Government does not agree with this recommendation.** People who enquire about potential entitlement to Universal Credit will be advised to make a claim immediately so that their entitlement can be properly determined. Universal Credit will be a dynamic online service that will allow claimants to make their claim as soon as they need. This increased access should mean that backdating is only required for claimants experiencing specific circumstances as set out in the regulations.

Conclusion

111. The Secretary of State would once again like to thank the Committee for its helpful report and recommendations and also to thank those who responded to the Committee's consultation.

112. Universal Credit represents the most significant reform of the welfare system in a generation. As such, the work the Department is doing to begin the implementation of Universal Credit in 2013 has generated significant interest amongst a range of stakeholders. The support provided by these stakeholders over the Autumn of 2012 has been vital in helping the Department develop Universal Credit in a way that can be delivered successfully.

113. The Secretary of State is pleased to be able bring forward regulations which address a number of the Committee's concerns and make improvements to the way in which Universal Credit will operate. These include the detailed arrangements for self-employed people, provisions to pay housing cost support for those living in supported exempt accommodation outside of Universal Credit, and provisions to provide alternative payment arrangements to support some claimants as they move to Universal Credit.

114. The Secretary of State is also pleased to accept the Committee's recommendations to monitor and evaluate the impact of the implementation of Universal Credit. Universal Credit marks a fundamental change to the way in which people engage with the benefit system and access in-work financial support. Its design, implementation and delivery will span a number of years. Comprehensive monitoring of delivery will be of critical importance to the implementation of Universal Credit as will the power to trial different approaches, if required, in the future.

115. The Department is assembling an expert advisory group to help with the evaluation of Universal Credit but the Secretary of State is confident that, in addition, the Social Security Advisory Committee will continue to offer its well considered views as Universal Credit is rolled out.

SSAC recommendations

Definitions and guidance

(i) The Government should ensure that its regulations and underpinning guidance contain clear, consistent and unambiguous definitions. The Committee would welcome an opportunity to comment on the draft guidance to ensure that it achieves this. *[Paragraph 2.5]*

Monitoring and evaluation

(ii) The Government should establish a robust monitoring mechanism and evaluation process to facilitate rapid and informed responses to emerging issues as Universal Credit is rolled out. The Committee would welcome the opportunity to provide support in shaping and monitoring these evaluation arrangements. *[Paragraph 2.7]*

IT development

(iii) The Government should consider carefully the impact of any amendments to the Universal Credit regulations on the IT delivery plans, particularly in terms of available resources and the potential for delay and errors. In particular, the Committee would be concerned if a significant number of additional manual processing steps were to be introduced in order to accommodate changes to the regulations, and would encourage the Government to consider carefully how and when the full implementation is best phased in to permit the optimum application of the new IT system.*[Paragraph 2.8]*

Self employed

(iv) The Government should engage further with self employed organisations and their service providers on their concerns about monthly reporting in order to identify how the concerns raised might be resolved. For example, there would be merit in exploring the degree to which quarterly reporting, with a requirement to submit the necessary records within 15 days of the end of that period, would work within the Universal Credit regime. *[Paragraphs 3.6]*

(v) The Government should give further consideration to a full reconciliation being undertaken at the end of the final quarter when gains and losses are properly balanced out and aligned with self assessment returns being submitted to HMRC. *[Paragraph 3.6]*

(vi) Given the concerns raised about the practicalities of the monthly reporting arrangements, the Government should consider piloting the arrangements with a sufficient number of self employed people to be truly representative before introducing any new arrangements in 2014.*[Paragraph 3.6]*

(vii) The inability to roll forward losses from an earlier assessment period is likely to disadvantage unfairly those self employed individuals and small businesses whose income flows are irregular and/or seasonal. The Committee recommends that this is looked at again. *[Paragraph 3.11*

(viii) The Government should reflect further on the list of exclusions from permitted expenses (for example, expenses 'incurred unreasonably', expenditure on cars, and interest payments). *[Paragraph 3.12]*

(ix) DWP and HMRC should move towards a unified reporting regime (with the timescales for implementation harmonised) that will both assist compliance and keep administrative burdens on small and 'start up' businesses to a minimum. *[Paragraph 3.17]*

(x) The Government should allow claimants more than one start-up period in a lifetime. The Prince's Trust has proposed that there should be a specified minimum period - say, three years - which must elapse before a further start-up period would be allowed. Given their considerable experience of supporting young people in establishing businesses, this suggestion should be explored further. *[Paragraph 3.22]*

(xi) The Government should give further consideration to the impact on industry groups likely to be disproportionately affected by the Universal Credit regulations, and to engage with them on developing innovative ways in which their concerns might be overcome. *[Paragraph 3.25]*

(xii) Given the potential impact of quasi self employment on vulnerable claimants, the Government should provide further clarity on the responsibilities of the Government, employers and their intermediaries, and individual jobseekers in determining the employment status of posts, in particular for the purpose of reporting income. *[Paragraph 3.28]*

(xiii) The Government should consider carefully the formal guidance that will be applied to the application of conditionality and the minimum income floor in cases where a claimant, while technically self-employed, is in fact in a situation of seeking work rather than developing a business. This will safeguard against those who are not developing a business being inadvertently treated by the Department as if they are. *[Paragraph 3.28]*

(xiv) Immediately prior to, and during the early implementation of, Universal Credit for the self employed, a level of discretion and system flexibility should be maintained to allow initial learning to be reflected in its application and thus avoid it being discredited by unintended outcomes. *[Paragraph 3.30]*

Housing

(xv) Given the inevitable tension between the position of landlords and tenants in terms of direct payments, and as only limited evidence is available about the likely behavioural impacts of the change, the Committee recommends that this is a particularly important area that the Government should keep under review, in particular by putting in place arrangements for effective monitoring and evaluation. *[Paragraph 4.5]*

(xvi) The Government should clarify the wording *'services necessary to maintain the fabric of the dwelling'* in the regulations. *[Paragraph 4.11]*

(xvii) Given the volume of responses received commenting on service charges, and the very wide variation in the potential impact described within them, it is not easy to identify where the eligibility line might most sensibly be drawn. However it is a clear area of concern for many and the Committee would urge the Government to engage quickly with key stakeholders, some of whom have acknowledged the need to simplify and streamline the existing rules, to discuss further whether the policy intention and practical consequences are sufficiently understood and aligned. *[Paragraph 4.11]*

(xviii) The Government should reflect further on the potential consequences of the under-occupancy proposals on the recently bereaved, disabled children and adults (including those with behavioural issues and overnight care needs); and on family members who are temporarily absent from the family home but where there is clear evidence that they will rejoin the family unit at some point in the near future. *[Paragraph 4.12]*

(xix) As a significant number of responses called for the provision of accommodation for those that need intensive and often specialised care and support to be taken out of the Universal Credit system, the Government should reflect on those concerns further in reaching detailed decisions on this sensitive area of policy. *[Paragraph 4.13]*

(xx) The Government should put arrangements in place to monitor and evaluate the impact of the Support for Mortgage Interest 'zero earnings rule'. *[Paragraph 4.15]*

(xxi) The Government should give further consideration to the issues that have been raised regarding the impact of the proposals on refuges for people fleeing the fear of violence, and engage directly with key stakeholders on the issue. *[Paragraph 4.17]*

Benefit Cap

(xxii) The Government should, in close co-operation with local authorities, undertake a robust monitoring and evaluation programme along the lines outlined in section 5 of this report, and to use it to inform any appropriate adjustments to the implementation of the overall benefits cap policy. In evaluating the effectiveness of this policy, the totality of costs to the taxpayer (whether through central or local government) should be considered rather than monitoring savings delivered to the Department's benefit expenditure in isolation. *[Paragraph 5.8]*

Sanctions
(xxiii) The Government should ensure that detailed guidance is directed towards ensuring that claimant commitment conditions are personalised for each claimant and are reasonable and achievable, taking all the claimant's circumstances into account. *[Paragraph 6.8]*

(xxiv) The Government should give consideration to the proposal that a sanction should be suspended when a claimant re-engages and terminated completely only after the claimant has been in work for a period of six months. The sanction could be re-instated if the claimant breaches their conditionality in that period. *[Paragraph 6.15]*

(xxv) In-work conditionality is clearly different to the kinds of conditions that will be placed on claimants that are out of work. The Government should consider introducing a separate regulation that deals with claimants who are in work to provide clarification of this difference. It should also consider a staged approach to developing in-work conditionality which is evidence based to ensure that the risk of negative impacts is minimised. *[Paragraph 6.18]*

(xxvi) The Government should undertake robust and comprehensive evaluation of the new sanction arrangements. The Committee is keen to assist in the design and development of this. *[Paragraph 6.22]*

Claims and Payments

(xxvii) The Government should consider establishing, on the basis of what it has learned from previous attempts to encourage a shift to on-line channels, a phased take-up over a transitional period. The aim should be to optimise the prospects of securing the maximum shift over time to on-line channels consistent with appropriate protection for vulnerable claimants. *[Paragraph 7.8]*

(xxviii) The Government should ensure that it has sufficient resources in place to support those claimants who are initially unable to make claims online because of capability or accessibility difficulties, to make claims by telephone or, where appropriate, through a home visit. *[Paragraph 7.8]*

(xxix) The content of information leaflets and guidance notes on making a claim on-line should be clear and unambiguous, using language that occasional computer users will readily understand. It should also explain what they should do to make a claim in the event that they are unable to do so on-line having followed that guidance. The Committee would welcome an opportunity to review and comment on drafts of any communications material being produced. *[Paragraph 7.8]*

(xxx) The Committee looks forward to receiving detailed proposals for the provision of education on financial management and the provision of other professional assistance to support people in moving from weekly to monthly budgets. It recommends that the Government should monitor the impact of this support to ensure that it is effective and responsive to the needs of claimants. *[Paragraph 7.14]*

(xxxi) The Committee welcomes the Government's intention to retain direct payment in some circumstances but, since the criteria will be set out in guidance, it would encourage the Government to consult landlords, their representatives and other stakeholders on its provisions. The Committee also looks forward to learning about the results of the social sector demonstration projects and urges the Department to take account of their findings. *[Paragraph 7.16]*

(xxxii) Clear guidance will be required on handling 'joint claims' where one member of a couple fails to make a 'claimant commitment'. The Government should also consider whether, in a limited number of cases, the claim may be processed for one member of the couple as a single person to avoid hardship. *[Paragraph 7.18]*

(xxxiii) The Government should ensure that the necessary arrangements are put in place to safeguard the confidentiality of personal details (particularly addresses) submitted by people who have been subject to domestic abuse. *[Paragraph 7.19]*

(xxxiv) The Government should retain 'good cause' provisions for back-dating in some limited cases, for example where a claimant has received misleading benefit advice. *[Paragraph 7.22]*

(xxxv) The Government should review its arrangements for communicating with those claimants who are less able to maintain their award on-line regularly, for example where they are relying on public access computers. The use of text message alerts or smart phone applications are options that should be explored. *[Paragraph 7.23]*

(xxxvi) The Government should reflect further on when payments are made in order to find a solution that accommodates the needs of claimants, the originators of direct debits, as well as its own needs for simplicity. *[Paragraph 7.24]*

SSAC report

Rt Hon Iain Duncan Smith

Secretary of State

Department for Work and Pensions

Caxton House

Tothill Street

London SW1H 9NA

23 August 2012

Dear Secretary of State

Universal Credit and related regulations

Given the unprecedented scale of the change to the welfare system that the Government is about to implement through the introduction of Universal Credit, we were pleased to have the opportunity to scrutinise, and consult on, the regulations. I am delighted to present our report to you.

The context within which the consultation was undertaken was challenging. The regulations on which we were seeking views were working drafts and, inevitably, contained gaps; and the period over which we were asking for evidence was - given the proposed legislative timetable - shorter than our normal consultation period. Despite this, the Committee received an unprecedented number of responses, and from a range of organisations and individuals that extended beyond our traditional group of stakeholders.

The majority of respondents were broadly supportive of the Government's ambitions to simplify the benefit system through the introduction of Universal Credit. The responses have, in the main, focused on the more practical aspects of its delivery, and on the impact it will have on a significant minority of groups and individuals that are perceived to be disadvantaged by the changes.

The Committee acknowledges that policy needs to be designed for the majority, and that many of the issues raised are probably not new to the Department. We hope, however, that the report will facilitate a reasoned debate between the Government and stakeholders about potential innovative solutions and transitional arrangements to address some of the concerns raised both prior to implementation and as Universal Credit is rolled out. The Committee feels that the widespread support for the overall principles of Universal Credit expressed during the consultation could be eroded if the Government does not show some flexibility in addressing the reasonable concerns that have been expressed.

Finally, I should like to record my thanks to the Department's officials who worked with Committee members and our secretariat in a supportive and collaborative way throughout the process.

Paul Gray
Chair

SOCIAL SECURITY
ADVISORY COMMITTEE

UNIVERSAL CREDIT AND RELATED REGULATIONS

August 2012

Introduction

1.1.   The Welfare Reform Act 2012 sets out the overall framework for Universal Credit. The implementation of these arrangements will require the passage of several sets of detailed regulations.

1.2.   The draft *Universal Credit Regulations 2012* and *Benefit Cap (Housing Benefit) Regulations 2012* are not subject to statutory referral to the Committee as it is planned that they will be made within six months of the commencement of the relevant enabling power. However, in recognition of the magnitude of the changes encompassed by these measures, the Secretary of State for Work and Pensions invited the Social Security Advisory Committee (SSAC) to consider them in a similar way to regulations that are subject to formal scrutiny under the Social Security Administration Act 1992.

1.3.   The Committee considered these, alongside the *Universal Credit, Personal Independence Payment and Working-age Benefits (Claims and Payments) Regulations 2012*, which the Department had submitted for formal scrutiny as required by the 1992 Act, at its meeting on 13 and 14 June 2012, during which it decided to consult a broad range of organisations and individuals on the regulations.

1.4.   The Government's legislative timetable required the Committee to complete its consultation on the draft regulations within a shorter period of time than usual - just eight weeks. That, combined with the comprehensive and broad-ranging nature of the regulations being considered, meant that the Committee focussed primarily on those aspects of the regulations that had not already been subject to scrutiny and debate during the passage of - and which are not embodied in - the Welfare Reform Act 2012.

1.5.   The Committee has also been particularly keen to examine the coherence of the package of regulations in terms of implementation, and whether there are gaps and/or unintended consequences that need to be addressed.

1.6.   The regulations published for consultation on 16 June were a working draft and DWP officials have continued to develop and refine them throughout the consultation period. The Committee has restricted its comments to that original draft of the regulations and, inevitably, some of the issues the Committee has reported on have been overtaken by events. A letter to the Committee Secretary from Charlotte Wightwick (Deputy Director, Universal Credit) on 3 August (attached at annex A) outlines the changes made during the consultation period.

1.7.   The Committee has received an unprecedented level of responses (just under 400) to its consultation exercise. The Committee was particularly pleased to note that submissions have been made by a wide variety of organisations and individuals extending beyond the Committee's traditional group of stakeholders (a full list of respondents is attached at annex B). We are grateful for the time that they have committed to producing thoughtful and informative responses.

1.8.   The majority of responses to this consultation can be categorised as falling within the following five broad themes:

- self employment;
- housing;
- the benefit cap;
- sanctions; and
- claims and payments.

1.9.   This report addresses each theme in turn in the sections that follow. The conclusions and recommendations of the Committee are summarised in section 8 of this report.

1.10. The Committee also received a number of very detailed comments about the regulations and, given their largely technical nature, the Committee Secretary has written separately to Departmental officials about these points.

2. Overarching issues

2.1.   In considering several sets of regulations, a number of overarching issues have arisen that are common to them all. These are set out below.

Definitions / consistency

2.2.   In line with the Government's commitment to promoting alternatives to regulation, primary and secondary legislation on social security is increasingly becoming a means of securing a broad policy objective, with the detail on how that will be achieved outlined in underpinning enabling guidance. Given that this will inform benefit decisions which have statutory force, it is important that the guidance - and its fit with the parent/related legislation - is subject to the same level of scrutiny.

2.3.   It will be particularly important to ensure that the definitions provided in the Department's legislation and enabling guidance are clear and unambiguous. The Committee has observed that some terms used - for example the parallel use of 'renter', 'joint renter' and 'tenant' - do not have clear legal definitions where it would expect one to exist, and that some which do are used in a way that does not appear to accord with that legal definition. If the terminology is not properly defined, it is foreseeable that appeal cases could succeed at tribunals.

2.4.   A further example of this, which many respondents have highlighted, is the lack of a definition for the term 'vulnerable'. The Department has said that it will provide exceptions for 'vulnerable claimants', but there will inevitably be individuals who consider themselves to be vulnerable but to whom those exceptions will not apply. It is important, therefore, that clarity is provided on where the lines will be drawn in terms of vulnerability.

2.5.   For these reasons, the Committee would welcome the opportunity to comment on the draft guidance being produced by the Department. The Committee considers it important that there is clarity and certainty for DWP staff, claimants and advisors, and therefore welcomes the Department's commitment to continue to make its guidance for decision-makers publicly available.

Recommendation 1: The Government should ensure that its regulations and underpinning guidance contain clear, consistent and unambiguous definitions. The Committee would welcome an opportunity to comment on the draft guidance to ensure that it achieves this.

Monitoring and evaluation

2.6.   Universal Credit is a radical approach to welfare reform and, because of that, it is transformational rather than evolutionary. It is therefore inevitable that, at this stage of the process, there is less certainty about the impact of specific measures on certain groups, particularly when one of the aims is to generate behavioural change. This also means that it is hard reliably to forecast the Departmental resources required for particular roles and difficult to draft comprehensive guidance notes that anticipate all the issues that may arise.

2.7.   The Committee is, therefore, of the firm view that it will be crucial to the credibility of Universal Credit as it rolls out that adequate monitoring and evaluation is in place to allow rapid and informed responses to emerging issues. Some of the consequences of the reform will inevitably be unforeseen and unwelcome for a minority, and these cases are almost certain to generate disproportionate attention from the media and lobby groups. The right data collection and reporting framework needs to be put in place from the outset.

Recommendation 2: The Committee recommends that the Government establishes a robust monitoring mechanism and evaluation process to facilitate rapid and informed responses to emerging issues as Universal Credit is rolled out. The Committee would welcome the opportunity to provide support in shaping and monitoring these evaluation arrangements.

IT development

2.8. The Committee understands that the development of the IT to support Universal Credit has been based on the draft regulations on which this consultation was based, and that it is at an advanced stage. There is, therefore, a risk that changes to the draft regulations may impact on the IT delivery plan.

Recommendation 3: As a number of the regulations are still being developed, and the recommendations in this report may lead to further late amendments, the Committee recommends that the Government considers carefully the impact of any amendments on the IT delivery plans, particularly in terms of available resources and the potential for delay and errors. In particular, the Committee would be concerned if a significant number of additional manual processing steps were to be introduced in order to accommodate further changes to the regulations, and would encourage the Government to consider carefully how and when the full implementation is best phased in to permit the optimum application of the new IT system.

Cross-government issues

2.9. Inevitably, the introduction of Universal Credit will have implications for a number of other government departments in terms of policy, operational delivery and resources. It is, therefore, essential for the Department to continue to have discussions at a senior level to ensure that these implications are fully understood and, where risks are identified, appropriate mitigations put in place. The main issues identified by respondents are outlined below:

(a) IT inter-dependence: it is essential that the various government IT platforms that will be used to support the effective delivery of Universal Credit are stable, able to exchange data effectively and securely; and protected from external threats (eg cyber fraud). It is especially important to ensure that the security of personal information relating to particularly vulnerable individuals, for example those on the witness protection scheme, cannot be compromised.

(b) Alignment of government policies: it will be important to ensure that Universal Credit does not impact negatively on the policy aims of other government departments, for example the impact of Universal Credit on BIS[1] and HMRC's[2] policy objectives relating to the self employed and on small businesses needs to be considered; as does the interaction between Universal Credit and locally administered Council Tax Benefit. Respondents have also asserted that the benefit cap could have a negative impact on DCLG's[3] Troubled Families programme.

(c) Passported benefits: the way in which current 'passported' support will be made available by other government departments will be key in determining whether or not the Government's aim of reducing complexity and making work pay have been met. For example, the value of school meals and health costs are significant and careful thought should be given to how that support is shaped and

---

[1] Department for Business, Innovation and Skills
[2] HM Revenue and Customs
[3] Department for Communities and Local Government

delivered in future, drawing on the principles set out in the Committee's report on passported benefits[4].

(d) Impact on communities: respondents highlighted the potential for the reform to impact on local authorities who might find themselves faced with greater numbers of homeless families that require support through social services, for example as a result of migration of claimants from high cost to low cost housing areas (this is discussed further in section 5). This runs counter to the DCLG's policy for the prevention of homelessness.

(e) Resources: respondents noted that a number of organisations were likely to have higher demands on their services as a consequence of this reform at a time when they were facing a reduction in available resources, for example legal aid, libraries, transport in rural areas.

2.10. This list is not intended to be exhaustive, simply illustrative of the need for the Department to continue to explore the potential impacts of these reforms on other related policies with colleagues across Whitehall and in local government.

European law

2.11. The Universal Credit regulations are bringing together in a unified framework the legislative arrangements for a range of benefits which currently attract different treatments under European Union (EU) law. Depending on their nature, benefits can be classified as 'social security', 'special non contributory benefits' or 'social assistance' for the purposes of EU Co-ordination Law EC Regulations 883/04 and 1408/71.

---

[4] Social Security Advisory Committee: *Passporting to the future: the SSAC review of passported benefits* (March 2012) http://www.dwp.gov.uk/docs/ssac-rev-of-pass-bens.pdf

2.12. The Committee understands that the breadth of the circumstances attracting support within Universal Credit means that classification of the unified benefit is not straightforward. The Committee also recognises that the classification has important ramifications governing access to and exportability of benefits.

2.13. In that context, some respondents to the consultations have questioned the proposed classification of all aspects of Universal Credit as social assistance. The Committee recognises the force of these submissions and views these as important questions, and suggests this is an issue the Department may wish to consider further.

3. Self employed

3.1. Respondents to this aspect of the consultation have widely welcomed the Government's commitment to:

- encouraging self employment as a route to economic independence and a contribution to overall national economic growth;
- simplifying and reducing burdens on business; and
- encouraging fuller take up of benefit entitlements.

3.2. However, they have also highlighted a number of areas in which it appears that these ambitions may not be realised, and which could create:

- increased administrative burdens, greater complexity and higher costs for the self-employed person seeking to set up a new business; and

- a disincentive to low income self employed individuals to claim Universal Credit even though they have an entitlement.

3.3. The responses submitted to the consultation have come from self employed individuals and accountants, as well as organisations representing them. The vast majority of submissions are consistent in terms of the concerns raised, and these have been drawn together comprehensively in the submissions received from the Low Income Tax Reform Group, the Institute of Chartered Accountants in England and Wales, and the Chartered Institute of Taxation.

Monthly reporting

3.4. The requirement for the self employed to report their earnings in monthly assessment periods, and within seven days of the end of that assessment period, is considered to be impractical by the majority of respondents. An individual's ability to prepare full and accurate records within these timescales could potentially be impaired by a number of factors outside their direct control. For example:

(a) *Bank statements*: the experience of many respondents is that bank statements rarely arrive within seven days of the end of the month to which they refer.

(b) *Book-keepers*: there is a concern about the capacity of book-keepers who represent a large number of self employed clients and whether they would be able to meet these additional reporting requirements within such a tight deadline.

(c) *Family support*: many self employed individuals depend on a partner or family member to manage their administrative affairs. In the event of a bereavement, relationship breakdown or more every day domestic event (for example going on holiday), this support can be lost and it is very unlikely that the self employed person will be able to remedy the loss within a short period of time.

(d) *Availability*: the ability of the small business owner to prepare the accounts within the deadline will be compromised when they are suffering from an illness, managing high business demands, or are travelling.

> *... there is a compromise to be made between responsiveness of the system for calculating self-employed benefits and the burden imposed upon those businesses in providing the information to underpin the calculations. Self-employed individuals who are in receipt of Universal Credit are not going to be in a position to engage regular professional assistance in preparing their books and records. Nor will they wish to devote any more time than is strictly necessary to non-profit making activities, and so while completing Universal Credit claims may be essential, the process must be as quick and simple as possible, imposing the minimum incremental burden on claimants.*
>
> *For many small businesses, the proposed timetable for self-reporting will not be achievable. ACCA has received expressions of concern from members, for example, "I have many very small business clients and know, without a shadow of doubt, that they will be unable to comply with the monthly reporting required under Universal Credits."*
>
> **Association of Chartered Certified Accountants**
> **(submission to SSAC consultation, August 2012)**

3.5.   Additionally, there is a concern that the combination of monthly reporting and a seven day deadline could lead to a greater number of errors or misreporting when claimants are under pressure to complete returns without all necessary information being readily available, exposing genuine claimants to the risk of being judged negligent or even fraudulent.

3.6.   The suspension of payments for failing to comply with this requirement is considered by many of the respondents to be overly harsh given the degree of challenge involved in preparing the accounts.

Recommendation 4: In view of the strength of the evidence submitted, the Committee recommends that the Government engages further with the self employed and their service providers on this issue in order to identify how these concerns might be resolved. For example, there would be merit in exploring the degree to which quarterly reporting, with a requirement to submit the necessary records within 15 days of the end of that period, would work within the Universal Credit regime.

Recommendation 5: Further thought should also be given to a full reconciliation being undertaken at the end of the final quarter when gains and losses are properly balanced out and aligned with self assessment returns being submitted to HMRC.

Recommendation 6: Given the concerns raised about the practicalities of the monthly reporting arrangements, the Committee would recommend that the Government pilots the arrangements with a sufficient number of self employed people to be truly representative before introducing any new arrangements in 2014.

Permitted expenses

3.7.   Regulation 54(1) defines permitted expenses as:

> *'amounts paid in the assessment period for expenses that have been wholly and exclusively incurred for the purposes of that trade profession or vocation...'.*

3.8.   While the regulation generally follows the same basis for deduction as for tax, respondents identified a number of divergences which merit further consideration.

3.9. In particular, the exclusion of rolling forward losses from an earlier assessment period was an area of concern among the consultation respondents. While they recognised the need to provide a snapshot of actual income and expenditure in a given assessment period, the respondents were concerned that small businesses would incur losses for which there would never be any recognition. For example, a number of respondents noted that payment of income tax and Class 4 National Insurance contributions, which are payable in two instalments in a given year, would be recognised but if the income received in that period was insufficient to cover the payment there would be no provision for carrying forward the loss or offsetting it against the other months to which the payment applied.

3.10. Such a case would create a distorted view of how a business is performing in economic terms. The Government acknowledged this point when the Welfare Reform Act 2012 was being considered in its Committee stage by the House of Commons:

> *In the end, this will all have to be evened out. There will have to be a proper assessment at the end of the year of what a self-employed person's income was and the amount of universal credit they received... There will be a point of reckoning, to work out whether we paid too much or too little. The system will clearly be in the interests of those who are claiming. One reason for introducing the self-reporting mechanism is to ensure that our information is as timely as possible, so that we do not end up in the mess we ended up in with the tax credit system. Where possible, the final figures will be as close to being right as is feasible.*
>
> **Hansard (Column 526)**
> **26 April 2011**

3.11. The proposed annual reconciliation outlined by the Government does not feature in the draft regulations. While annual reconciliation would, in itself, create further administrative burdens for the self employed, that would be preferable to the position outlined in the draft regulations which does not allow for losses in unprofitable assessment periods to be evened out against gross profit in others.

Recommendation 7: The inability to roll forward losses from an earlier assessment period is likely to disadvantage unfairly those self employed individuals and small businesses whose income flows are irregular and/or seasonal. The Committee recommends that this is looked at again as this will be seen as inherently unfair and it may lead to formal challenges and claimants seeking ways to get around the reporting requirements as set out.

3.12. Other exclusions from the definition of permitted expenses which respondents argue merit further consideration are:

(a)   Expenses 'incurred unreasonably': there is no precedent for this in the tax system and greater clarification of what it means, and the mechanism for determining whether an expense is unreasonable, is required. The cheapest option for a particular business expense might not represent the best value for money nor be the best option for valid commercial reasons. This could lead to poor business decisions being made for fear of a cost being retrospectively judged 'unreasonable'.

(b)   Expenditure on cars: given that expenditure on vans is permitted[5], the proposal seems arbitrarily to discriminate against those businesses where the use of a car is essential (for example, taxi drivers, or driving instructors) or more economical (for example, providing domestic or personal services where no significant

---

[5] regulation 54(2)(d)

equipment needs to be carried) and creates an ambiguity between vans, often designed to be suitable for private use as well as business use.

(c)   Interest payments: respondents could not readily understand why interest payments are excluded but hire purchase costs are not. There is a view that this would simply incentivise small businesses to source equipment and other goods through hire purchase rather than bank loans when establishing a new business.

Recommendation 8: **The Committee recommends that the list of exclusions from permitted expenses is an issue on which the Government should reflect further.**

Alignment with HM Revenue and Customs

3.13.   Respondents to the consultation made strong representations about the lack of consistency in reporting requirements between HMRC and DWP which inevitably compromises the spirit of simplification and places additional burdens on small businesses and the self employed.

3.14.   The Office of Tax Simplification's report *'Simpler income tax for the smallest businesses: a discussion paper'* also recognised this as a potential issue for the Government to consider:

> *If an alternative system for calculating tax (and NI) liabilities is adopted, it is essential that the regime used for tax is also accepted for other purposes, such as claiming welfare benefits. It would not only negate any simplification if claimants needed to keep different records and calculate income in different ways for tax and Universal Credit, it would add to complexity.*
>
> **Small businesses tax review: simpler income tax**
> **for the smallest business (paragraph 4.34)**

3.15. HMRC's consultation *'Simpler income tax for the simplest small businesses'*, which sought views on the merits of a 'cash basis' of accounting for businesses with a turnover of up to £77,000 per annum, ended on 22 June 2012. The consultation document made clear that HMRC would work with DWP to identify how it might be possible to align aspects of the cash basis accounting for tax and self employment income reporting for Universal Credit.

3.16. The response to that consultation has yet to be published (it is anticipated that draft legislation will be published in autumn 2012), but the cash basis accounting on which it sought views is different from that described in the Universal Credit regulations in a number of respects, for example:

(a) Under the HMRC proposals, a loss in one period may be carried forward and set against profit in another period; as noted earlier, the Universal Credit regulations do not allow for this type of 'carry forward'.

(b) Refunds or repayments of Income Tax, Value Added Tax (VAT) and National Insurance contributions are included as receipts of the trade for Universal Credit purposes; HMRC excludes 'refunds of income tax, capital gains tax or tax credits', but includes VAT.

(c) Expenditure on cars is excluded in favour of mileage allowances for the purposes of Universal Credit; HMRC additionally excludes expenditure on motorcycles which Universal Credit does not.

(d) DWP's rules allow vans and other vehicles apart from cars to claim for the expenses of purchase as well as using the fixed rate mileage allowances; under HMRC rules it is one or the other, but not both.

(e)   The treatment of flat rate deductions where a person uses their home for business purposes is handled differently by each department; HMRC proposes a three-tiered banded adjustment to allow for private use, whereas DWP proposes three flat rates depending on the number of hours spent on income-generating activities in each assessment period.

> *Small businesses currently have to prepare accounts on which their direct tax returns are based, and separately keep records for VAT. ACCA is disappointed that DWP and HMRC have not committed to using the same simplified methodology for small businesses, whether they are calculating what they owe to the state, or what the state owes to them. The mismatch between the two will serve only to confuse those for whom form filling and officialdom is already a significant burden, and for no apparent advantage.*
>
> *Whatever scheme is adopted for simplified record keeping for small business, it should be uniform as far as possible across all that business's dealings with the state. Quite apart from the risks of unfairness where individuals are expected to pay their taxes based on different figures to those which determine the level of benefits to which they are entitled, it seems counterintuitive to deliberately introduce further complexity to the bureaucratic burden faced by small business in the UK.*
>
> **Association of Chartered Certified Accountants**
> **(submission to SSAC consultation, August 2012)**

3.17. The clear view of respondents to the consultation in relation to this issue was that the proposals outlined in the draft regulations would create a disproportionate burden on the smallest businesses whose proprietors are most likely to apply for Universal Credit. This would be exacerbated by any non-alignment between reporting dates (defined by the date of claim) and the calendar month end.

Recommendation 9: The Committee recommends that DWP and HMRC moves towards a unified reporting regime (with the timescales for implementation harmonised) that will both assist compliance and keep administrative burdens on small and 'start up' businesses to a minimum.

Minimum Income Floor

3.18. Respondents welcomed the idea of a start-up period in which the minimum income floor would not be applied, and cited examples of successful businesses that would have struggled to reach an assumed level of income after just one year since much of that first year is spent developing the business to get it to a point where it can begin trading. It is also likely that in order for a business to succeed, a substantial amount of the takings will need to be reinvested into the business during that period. A Prince's Trust survey of successful businesses gave several examples of this.

Zoe My business turned a profit of just over £5,000 in its first year – but this was reinvested in moving into business premises and buying more expedition kit. At the start of year two I decided the business could afford to pay me £300 per month and was able to increase this to £750 per month after another 6 months. Finally 22 months after starting the business I was able to pay myself above minimum wage for the first time. I am now a higher-rate taxpayer, provide year round work for 4 other staff and contract 50 more freelance employees who help deliver our work. The income I received from Working Tax Credit was a real lifeline.

Prince's Trust survey of its
network of successful businesses
(submission to SSAC consultation, August 2012)

> **Chris** *I wasn't earning the minimum wage for the first two years of trading. Income was up and down every month... Working Tax Credit has been a life saver – especially in the early days and more recently when income has dropped off in the business.*
>
> **Prince's Trust survey of its**
> **network of successful businesses**
> **(submission to SSAC consultation, August 2012)**

3.19. In the absence of any detail during the consultation on the level of the minimum income floor, respondents urged ministers to consult small and medium enterprises, and their representative organisations, on this before any final decisions are taken. Some respondents assumed, for the purposes of the consultation, that the level of the minimum income floor would be closely aligned to the conditionality requirements for employed claimants – that of partaking in, or looking for, work for full-time hours at the national minimum wage. In the event that this became the Department's stated position, respondents would be concerned that many viable businesses would struggle to achieve it and would recommend that the start-up period was extended to a minimum of two years.

3.20. There were also widespread concerns about the proposal to restrict an individual to being eligible for only one start-up period in a lifetime. This could discourage an individual from having another try at starting a business if they had just one previously failed attempt, and could also deter young entrepreneurs from using their start-up period in their first effort at self employment. It fails to acknowledge that many successful entrepreneurs gain valuable lessons from initial failures.

3.21. There were also concerns about the lack of a provision to carry over the 'unspent' part of a start-up period if an individual recognises after a month or so that their business plan is not viable but subsequently wants to try again with a different approach.

3.22. This proposal was therefore considered to be counter-productive to the Government's efforts to develop the enterprise culture of the UK through initiatives such as the Business in You campaign and the enterprise loans scheme. The European Commission[6] has acknowledged that business entry and business exit are natural processes that are inherent to economic life, and that 50 per cent of enterprises in Europe do not survive the first five years. Research also suggests that, as asserted above, these organisations and individuals learn from their mistakes and those that re-start have lower rates of failure and experience faster growth in terms of turnover and jobs created than newly established companies[7].

Recommendation 10: The Committee recommends that the Government should allow claimants more than one start-up period in a lifetime. The Prince's Trust has proposed that there should be a specified minimum period - say, three years – which must elapse before a further start-up period would be allowed. Given their considerable experience of supporting young people in establishing businesses, this suggestion should be explored further.

Impact on specific industry groups

3.23. The Committee received a number of submissions outlining concerns about the potentially damaging impact that the Universal Credit regulations could have on particular industries within the UK. The most

---

[6] European Commission for Enterprise and Industry (January 2011) *Final Report of the Expert Group*

[7] Stam E., Audretsch D. B. and Meijaard J. ERIM (2006) *Renascent Entrepreneurship*

comprehensive submissions, which outlined the potential impact on the farming community, were received from the National Farmers Union and the Royal Agricultural Benevolent Institution.

3.24. In excess of 90 per cent of farmers in England and Wales are self employed; with between 31-43 per cent of all farmers earning less than the national minimum wage over the past five years[8]. But respondents have argued that it would be too simplistic to suggest that a third of all farmers should be seeking alternative work without considering the following factors:

(a)   The range of factors beyond a farmer's control (including external interventions, for example the weather) that affect the profitability of a farm.

(b)   The introduction of an assumed minimum income floor will remove a safety net at the point when farmers need help most; very few farming businesses are self sufficient before the end of the first year of operation. It is also likely to impact their ability to continue to employ workers; or result in farmers leaving the industry which may also mean the loss of their family home.

(c)   The consequences of the inability to roll forward losses from one accounting period to the next are exacerbated for the farming community where it is not uncommon to have a negative cash flow for 8-9 months a year with virtually the entire income being confined to a short 3-4 month period when the farm's produce is sold. The argument for an annual reconciliation exercise is very persuasive in this respect.

---

[8] Parliamentary Question (28 February 2012) Hansard (Column 193W)

3.25. Similar representations were made on behalf of freelance journalists who might work on developing a story for many months before it is ready to be pitched, published and paid for, and where weekly working hours and the predictability of eventual income are major variables. There may be other industry groups particularly affected from whom we have not received submissions.

Recommendation 11: **The Committee would encourage the Government to give further consideration to the impact on industry groups likely to be disproportionately affected by these regulations, and to engage with them on developing innovative ways in which their concerns might be overcome.**

Quasi self employment

3.26. Several respondents made reference to employers or employment intermediaries who engage people on the basis that they will be regarded as self employed, without making that sufficiently clear to the individual. An example provided to the Committee outlined a scenario where an individual would report to DWP that they had gained employment and provide the 'employer's' details, but the employer would make no 'real time information' (RTI) return for them and subsequently advise DWP that they were self-employed thus leading to loss of Universal Credit payments.

3.27. There was also concern that claimants would feel compelled to take up employment on self employed terms for fear of facing further action from the Department.

> *... employers treat them as self-employed, even though the relationship between the worker and the engager is in reality, strictly and probably legally, one of employment. The workers have no real choice in the matter – either they work for that employer on those terms, or they look elsewhere for work and face whatever sanctions are imposed for failure to take up the work that is offered...*
>
> **Low Income Tax Reform Group**
> **(submission to SSAC consultation, August 2012)**

3.28. Committee members saw for themselves a number of 'jobs' being advertised on 'self employed' terms during their visit to Streatham Jobcentre on 8 August 2012. This practice appears to be most common in casual or temporary employment and often involves the more vulnerable and lower paid. This has the potential to lead to an inadvertent loss of entitlement to Universal Credit.

Recommendation 12: Given the potential impact on vulnerable claimants, the Committee recommends that the Government provides further clarity on the responsibilities of the Government, employers and their intermediaries, and individual jobseekers in determining the employment status of posts, in particular for the purpose of reporting income.

Recommendation 13: The Committee also recommends the Government consider carefully the formal guidance that will be applied to the application of conditionality and the minimum income floor in cases where a claimant, while technically self-employed, is in fact in a situation of seeking work rather than developing a business. This will safeguard against those who are not developing a business being inadvertently treated by the Department as if they are.

Other Issues

3.29. Other issues raised during the consultation about self employment which the Committee would urge the Department to reflect on further are:

(a) *Part time work*: many people choose to combine self employment with part-time work, especially during a start-up period, and this is a practice that should be encouraged. However concerns were expressed that rules concerning minimum hours of work under Universal Credit were insufficiently flexible to support this approach to achieving greater economic independence.

(b) *Impact on the most vulnerable*: a number of respondents were of the view that Universal Credit does not adequately acknowledge the challenges faced by the most vulnerable, including those with a disability, who find themselves pursuing self employment not as a matter of choice but out of necessity as other forms of employment have proved impossible to secure. For them the challenges of understanding and complying with the requirements of Universal Credit will require high standards of communication and individual support from Jobcentre Plus and private welfare to work providers. There was also some concern that members of this group could be encouraged to attempt self employment despite it being an unsuitable option or having little likelihood of becoming a viable enterprise within the start-up period.

3.30. In conclusion, it is especially evident from the range of responses to the consultation that, while a simplified and universal benefit system is very widely welcomed, it also needs to be recognised that the range of people, capabilities and working patterns of self employed people are as broad and diverse as the overall labour market.

<u>Recommendation 14</u>: The Committee recommends that, immediately prior to, and during the early implementation of, Universal Credit for the self employed, a level of discretion and system flexibility is maintained to allow initial learning to be reflected in its application and thus avoid it being discredited by unintended outcomes.

4. Housing

4.1. The principle underlying Universal Credit that individual claimants should take more responsibility for their own financial affairs is reflected in the provisions below.

Tenants' responsibility for Housing Costs

4.2. Tenants will be handed back responsibility for their rent and stricter criteria will be applied when considering whether rental payments should be made directly to landlords.

4.3. The issue of direct payments has been a thorny policy area since the days of supplementary benefits. Experience has shown that significant numbers of claimants have deductions made from benefits towards payment of rent. It is understandable therefore that, given a substantive reform of the benefit system, the Government should wish to make the gateway far tighter. At present, a local authority is obliged to make direct payments to a landlord where arrears of rent have reached a figure equating to eight weeks rent, or if rent direct has been requested by the claimant and is considered to be in the family's best interests. This is a wide gateway. Claimants who rely upon direct payments tend to be long term benefit recipients and direct payments may act as a disincentive to find work.

4.4. The responses to the consultation have demonstrated equally understandable concerns about the proposed changes for landlords and claimants. Responses received make clear that there could be an increasing reluctance for landlords to let property to benefit claimants unless there is a degree of certainty that they will receive rent on time. Landlords report that there are already signs that this is happening in high-rent areas where demand for housing is strong and where the impact of recent cuts in housing benefit is beginning to be felt. Local authorities have also commented on this point. Although their statutory duty to house homeless people does not apply where the tenant has accumulated rent arrears and can be treated as voluntarily homeless, this particular rule does not apply if the reason for the arrears is attributable to the benefit cap or other savings measures. This has the potential to lead to a significant outlay on the part of the relevant authority for temporary accommodation.

The provision of housing is a relatively high risk venture, often dependent on the stability of income streams in order to meet additional financial commitments connected to the provision of accommodation….

…without recourse to establishing direct payment to the landlord where necessary, providers of commercial finance are likely to determine that the risk of lending is too high resulting in high costs to the borrower or a reduction in availability. This reduced availability and increased potential cost of provision will have a detrimental impact downstream on tenants…

…should a recipient of Universal Credit fail to pass on the relevant housing component to their housing provider for a period exceeding two months, the majority of landlords will be compelled to initiate possession proceedings in order to bring the tenancy to an end. This can often be avoided by the switch to direct payment to landlord.

…failure to control rent arrears through a coherent mechanism will lead to increased tenancy failure and recourse to possession proceedings which benefit neither party.

National Landlords Association
(submission to SSAC consultation, August 2012)

4.5.   The Committee was also advised that the exemption from the statutory duty to house the homeless will make for a grey area of decision-making as to why a person has accumulated rent arrears. Arguments against giving tenants on benefit greater financial responsibilities have also been made from the claimant's point of view.

Recommendation 15: There is an inevitable tension between the two positions outlined above and, as yet, limited evidence about the likely behavioural impacts of the change. Therefore, the Committee recommends that this is a particularly important area for the Government to keep under review, in particular by putting in place arrangements for effective monitoring and evaluation.

Service charges

4.6.   The current Housing Benefit (HB) rules allow for a large number of charges to be included within the amount of HB to which an individual may be entitled. They include the following:

- cleaning of the exterior of windows where neither the claimant nor any member of the household can do so;
- cleaning of rooms and windows in communal areas;
- provision of premises or equipment for personal laundry needs;
- provision and maintenance of a children's play area.
- charges for installing and maintaining radio and television equipment;
- a specified amount for meals; and
- provision of furniture that will not become the property of the claimant.

4.7.   The rules will be more restrictive under Universal Credit. For claimants renting a property within the social rented or privately rented sector, service charges will be included as housing costs only if its payment is a condition of occupation, and the services are:

- necessary to maintain the fabric of the accommodation;

- for the cleaning of communal areas; or

- the cleaning of the exterior of windows where neither the renter nor any member of the renter's extended benefit unit is able to clean them.

4.8. The Committee received a large number of responses on this aspect of the Universal Credit regulations, both in terms of the impact on tenants and on those organisations providing the services.

A large social landlord operating in the North West of England with around 11,500 properties spends:

- *£400,000 on fuel (lighting etc) for communal areas. Charges apply to around 4,300 tenants for this service but it still carries a loss of £200,000*

- *£700,000 on caretaker services for 2,200 tenants*

- *£500,000 on grounds maintenance for which 7,000 tenants are charged but it still carries a deficit of around £55,000*

Under the current system, the landlord carries a cost of £255,000 which is not covered by tenants' housing benefit. Under the Universal Credit system, the landlord would need to absorb £1,600,000 as none of these charges would be covered in tenants' Universal Credit claims. We believe these services are an important component of good housing and property management that are legitimately considered as a core component of benefit support to cover housing costs.

Example provided by the
Chartered Institute of Housing
(submission to SSAC consultation, August 2012)

> *Services that...would become ineligible under draft regulations could include communal utilities, council tax, gardening and a communal TV aerial. These services cost a total of £14.23 per client per week. Clients would also continue to have to pay £10.00 for service charges that are currently ineligible and would remain so under Universal Credit. This would mean that, in total, clients would pay £24.23 for service charges each week – an increase of over 142 per cent. Clients would find it extremely difficult to meet these extra costs.*
>
> **St Mungo's**
> **(submission to SSAC consultation, August 2012)**

4.9.   Although in some cases the service charge is a minor subsidiary of the main rent and can reasonably be expected to come from the tenant's other income, respondents suggest that in many other cases it forms a significant proportion of the rent and is critical in terms of its function. The balance between services and rent has, in more recent times, shifted towards services provided by the social rented sector. This has been due to:

(a)   *Legislative changes*: for example the need to ensure properties are accessible to disabled people and to provide an external smoking area.

(b)   *Motability scooters*: the increased usage of motability scooters which require secure storage.

(c)   *Technological advances*: for example, the advent of solar panels and increasing reliance upon CCTV and other security measures.

4.10. Respondents have also commented that as there are limits on the amount by which registered providers and housing associations can increase rents, some have relied on additional service charges to finance improvements to accommodation.

4.11. The clear concern outlined in many of the consultation responses is that vulnerable people will not be able to sustain their tenancies if these services are withdrawn or if tenants are required to pay for the services themselves. Additionally, there is a general view that greater clarification is required of the phrase *'services necessary to maintain the fabric of the dwelling'* which is used in the legislation. It could be interpreted and applied inconsistently across the country, and it could be some time before a clear definition emerges from case-law. In the meanwhile, smaller social housing providers are concerned that the financial viability of their organisation could be put at risk.

Recommendation 16: The Committee has already highlighted a need for clear definitions earlier in this report, so supports the view that the Government should clarify the wording *'services necessary to maintain the fabric of the dwelling'* in the regulations.

Recommendation 17: Given the volume of responses received commenting on this issue, and the very wide variation in the potential impacts described within them, it is not easy to identify where the eligibility line might most sensibly be drawn for service charges. However, it is a clear area of concern for many and the Committee would urge the Government to engage quickly with key stakeholders, some of whom have acknowledged the need to simplify and streamline the existing rules, to discuss further whether the policy intention and practical consequences are sufficiently understood and aligned.

Under-occupancy

4.12. The Department has recently introduced legislation which, from April 2013, will limit the amount of housing benefit to be paid where a tenant is deemed to have more bedrooms than required. This arrangement will be carried forward into Universal Credit. There are, inevitably, a number of exemptions where the under-occupancy rules will be disapplied or adjusted, either temporarily or permanently. The following exemptions have been the main focus of the comments received from respondents:

(a) *Bereavement*: the current 52-week period of grace would be reduced to three months following the introduction of Universal Credit, and many respondents were of the view that expecting bereaved families to handle these two significant pressures simultaneously would place an unreasonable level of stress on them. The Committee is sympathetic to this view.

(b) *Disabled people*: requiring a disabled child, or a child with behavioural issues, to share a bedroom with a sibling has the potential to be detrimental to the overall well-being of both. In addition, respondents noted that some disabled children require overnight care which cannot always be met by a parent and that, in these cases, the provision of a room for a carer should be permitted. Indeed, a recent Court of Appeal case[9] involving severely disabled children requiring an overnight carer concluded that the rules on determining local housing allowances are, in this respect, in breach of Article 14 of the Human Rights Act. The Committee is pleased to note that local authorities have been allocated funding to meet this provision through discretionary housing payments, though it wonders whether an exemption in the regulations might be more straight forward and less costly in terms of administration.

---

[9] EWCA Civ 629, 15 May 2012

(c) *Temporary absences*: the removal of the housing element from claimants in hospital, a care home, a residential school or in local authority care for more than six months was also reported to be a cause of concern. There is potential for the under-occupancy rules to impact on families in cases where there is a realistic expectation that the absence from the household, while exceeding six months, will be temporary. Similarly, the temporary absence of a young person from home while they attend university has the potential to render the family home under-occupied and require the remaining family members to relocate. In both of these circumstances the absent family members are likely to find it difficult to rejoin the household at a later date. A number of respondents have noted that these rules have the potential to change the current trend of children leaving the family home increasingly later – a trend which has informed government policy which allows for a lower rate of benefit to be paid to the under-25s, and the Committee considers that this is an unintended consequence that the Department might want to reflect on further.

Recommendation 18: The Committee suggests that the Government reflects further on the potential consequences of the under-occupancy proposals on the recently bereaved, disabled children and adults (including those with behavioural issues and overnight care needs); and on family members who are temporarily absent from the family home but where there is clear evidence that they will rejoin the family unit at some point in the near future.

Supported housing

4.13. Supported housing was another aspect of the regulations that attracted much comment. As this is an issue on which the Department continues to develop and refine its proposals, the majority of respondents were simply seeking further clarity of the Government's intention. There was, however, a significant number of responses which called for the provision of accommodation for those that need intensive and often specialised care and support to be taken out of the Universal Credit system altogether.

Recommendation 19: **The Committee would encourage the Government to take the concerns expressed fully into account in reaching detailed decisions on this sensitive area of policy.**

Support for Mortgage Interest – the 'zero earnings rule'

4.14. The intention within Universal Credit is that no help will be provided for owner-occupiers by way of support for mortgage interest repayments where the claimant, or either claimant in a couple case, are engaged in work. Crucially, in line with one of the key principles in Universal Credit, there is a 'no hours' rule as far as earnings are concerned. In other words, no help with the mortgage will be given when any kind of work is undertaken.

4.15. When this issue was first presented to the Committee, DWP officials provided an assurance that most owner-occupiers claiming an income-related benefit tend to be the first to find work and leave benefit. In practice, it was suggested to us that claimants in this situation do not venture into part-time work; either they are unable to work, in which case mortgage support will become available, or they will find full-time employment. The zero earnings rule was therefore described to the Committee as the best work incentive. Some respondents take a different view. For example, Gingerbread argue that this measure would be a disincentive for a single parent to take up part-time work that fits around their caring responsibilities. Newly separated parents staying in the family home are likely to want to minimise the upheaval for their children. Full-time employment may not be realistic in those circumstances and a consequence of that may be to edge them into rented accommodation where demand is already high.

We believe that the zero earnings rule attached to SMI is a disincentive for single parents to take up part-time work that fits around their caring responsibilities, and damages the aim of improving work incentives.

Gingerbread has welcomed the additional support for childcare for those in part-time work, which has the potential to enable single parent families to balance work and home life effectively, engage in the labour market, and move into full-time work. The zero earnings rule would make this much more difficult for those receiving SMI than those in the rented sector. The zero earnings rule not only creates a disincentive to move into work, but creates hard decisions for those currently working less than 16 hours per week and claiming SMI while doing so. With the help no longer available, single parents who cannot increase their hours, either because of their caring responsibilities or because of local labour market conditions, may have no choice but to stop work altogether.

It is an over simplification to assume that those claiming SMI have been in full-time work and intend to return to it. Single parents often want to stay in the same property if possible, and want to minimize the upheaval for their children after a separation.

Gingerbread
(submission to SSAC consultation, August 2012)

Recommendation 20: As with other aspects of these proposals, the Committee recommends that the Government puts arrangements in place to monitor and evaluate the impact of this proposal.

Refuges for people fleeing the fear of violence

4.16.   Almost a quarter of the total responses received were from organisations and individuals working in - or with - women's refuges. The majority of these formed part of a co-ordinated response. The main concern outlined in the submissions is that accommodation can only be offered to people fleeing violence, or the threat of it, on the basis of addressing an emergency. Sometimes the crisis can be very short-term, with those given temporary accommodation in a refuge being taken in by friends or relatives, or returning to home.

4.17.   Given the unpredictable nature of each potential crisis, the Universal Credit rules about changes of circumstances taking effect from the start of the monthly assessment period do not fit well. The draft regulations mean that an existing claimant arriving and leaving a refuge within their monthly assessment period would be entitled only to their regular monthly payment of benefit. The person or organisation providing the accommodation would receive nothing. Respondents were concerned that the network of support currently made available to those fleeing violence would be weakened.

Recommendation 21: The Committee recommends that the Government gives further consideration to the issues that have been raised, and engages directly with key stakeholders on the issue.

5. Benefit cap

5.1.   The Government propose to introduce a cap on total amount of benefit that working age claimants can receive so that households on out-of-work benefits cannot receive more than the national average weekly take-home wage.   Initially the cap will be administered by local authorities through Housing Benefit (HB) but, from October 2013, will be applied for all new claims to Universal Credit.   It is designed to:

- act as an incentive to work;
- promote greater fairness between those in receipt out of work benefits and those in work; and
- deliver a reduction in benefit expenditure.

Provision for a benefit cap

5.2.   Provision for a cap on working age benefits was set out in sections 96 and 97 of the Welfare Reform Act 2012.   The cap is designed to be a key component of the Universal Credit scheme, but in the interim is being applied to housing benefit (HB) in advance of the national roll out of Universal Credit.   The assessment of whether a particular claimant has reached or exceeded the cap will take into account a wide number of different benefits, however any reduction in benefit will be applied only to HB.   In cases where the amount of the reduction exceeds the available HB, benefit would be reduced only by that amount.

5.3.   These proposals were initially presented to the Committee at its meeting on 11 January 2012.   The Committee made the following recommendations during that discussion and these were subsequently accepted by the Government and draft regulations were amended accordingly:

(a)   Claimants in the ESA support group should be exempt from the cap.

(b)   A period of grace should be granted before applying the cap for people who had been made redundant.

(c)   Further funding should be made available to the Discretionary Housing Payment fund specifically for benefit cap cases (£120 million will be allocated to the fund over the two years 2013/2014 and 2014/15).

5.4.   The Committee considered the revised proposals at its meeting on 13 June 2012, during which it raised three further concerns:

(a)   The requirement to be engaged in remunerative work of 16 hours in the final week of work before the grace period of 39 weeks could apply.

(b)   The potential impact of the cap across a range of policy areas other than social security.

(c)   The implications for monitoring and evaluation of the impact of the cap and any necessary areas for mitigation.

5.5.   The concern in relation to the 16-hour rule in the final week of work resulted in a reconsideration of the policy. The Committee's view was that it could impact harshly where a claimant's hours in work are being wound down in the period before they are finally released from employment. In these circumstances someone who could only work part-time hours in their final week of work would be caught by the cap immediately upon claiming HB. Somebody else working full hours in their final week would have a grace period of 39 weeks before being subjected to the benefit cap. The Department consequently dropped the 16-hour requirement in the final week of work.

The potential impact of the cap

5.6.   The impact of this policy is inevitably untested since the legislation will not take effect until 2013, however the submissions received outline a number of potential areas of concern:

(a)   *Resources*: local authorities, in particular, are of the view that this policy will create high levels of additional demand on their resources. In evaluating the effectiveness of this policy, the Committee recommends that the totality of costs to the taxpayer (whether through central or local government) are considered alongside monitoring savings delivered to the Department's benefit expenditure in isolation.

(b)   *Communities*: some respondents were concerned that the potential migration of families on working age benefits to areas where housing costs are lower could lead to a reduction in mixed communities and lead to pockets of poverty, poor housing and increased social tension in some areas.

(c)   *Children*: the benefit cap is expected to have the greatest impact on large families, and respondents are concerned about the social costs of families being re-housed. Of the 50,000 households that the Department suggests will be impacted by the benefit cap, respondents estimate that 210,000 children will be affected, compared to around 70,000 adults.

> *... there will be large scale migration of affected families from more expensive parts of London to cheaper parts resulting in:-*
>
> - *Pressure on public services at a time of significantly reduced budgets.*
> - *An increase in the number of homelessness applications.*
> - *More demand and competition for limited housing which is really affordable.*
> - *Increased use of bed and breakfast accommodation.*
> - *Higher possession action from landlords.*
> - *The breakdown of mixed communities.*
> - *Difficulties in tracking the movement of vulnerable children and adults between boroughs.*
> - *Difficulties in tracking participants in government programmes between boroughs.*
>
> **London Councils**
> **(submission to SSAC consultation, August 2012)**

Monitoring and evaluating the cap

5.7. The Committee welcomes the steps taken by the Department and local authorities to alert individuals who are likely to be affected by the benefit cap about their options. The Committee is also pleased to see that it is the intention of the Department to monitor and evaluate the policy.

5.8. The Committee has identified a number of omissions from the topics which had been identified by the Department for evaluation and these are listed below, alongside other omissions identified during the consultation:

- Actual homelessness - beyond people being placed in temporary accommodation.

- Impact of the demand for housing and support via social services.

- Impacts to health, granted that the cap will apply to those people with medical conditions who are placed in the work-related activity group or who fall short of the 15 point threshold for the work capability assessment but still have significant impairments. These could include hospital admissions and suicide attempts.

- Repossession rates for rent arrears and homelessness applications to local authorities.

- Impact on other priority debts – for example, gas and electricity disconnection rates.

- Personal bankruptcies, debt relief orders and individual voluntary arrangements.

- Any increases in the rate and number of appeals against Employment and Support Allowance decisions from people who are trying to join the support group.

- Any increased numbers of applications for other qualifying benefits such as Disability Living Allowance (DLA), Personal Independence Payment (PIP) and Industrial Injuries Benefits.

- The inter-relation between the roll-out of PIP for existing DLA claimants and the benefit cap.

- Loss of jobs where people cannot continue to live in an area from which they can readily travel to work.

- The extent and amount of calls on discretionary housing payments to fill the gap.

- The impact on children in terms of schooling, anti-social behaviour, incidence of homeless and of children being taken into care.

Recommendation 22: **The Committee recommends that the Government, in close co-operation with local authorities, undertake a monitoring and evaluation programme on these lines wherever practicable, and use it to inform any appropriate adjustments to the implementation of the overall policy. In evaluating the effectiveness of this policy, the totality of costs to the taxpayer (whether through central or local government) should be considered rather than monitoring savings delivered to the Department's benefit expenditure in isolation.**

6. Sanctions

6.1.   A relatively small number of consultation respondents commented on the new conditionality and sanctions regimes within the Universal Credit regulations, noting the tougher approach to conditionality in which expectations of claimants are higher and sanctions for non-compliance appear more punitive. Most respondents recognised the importance of sanctions within the benefit system and welcomed the inclusion of the amount and duration of any sanction: this should result in a more effective sanctions regime. However the move to a tougher approach gave rise to a number of general observations:

(a)   An increasingly punitive system must be alive to the structural barriers to employment faced by some claimants, especially those living in poverty.

(b)   Sanctions may have positive impacts on job search activities but may result in unintended consequences, such as family breakdown or homelessness. Sanctions should not operate in a way which is counter-productive; for examples causing an individual to disengage from the system or reducing incentives to look for paid employment.

(c)   A tougher approach requires an understanding of and a sensitivity to the challenges faced by vulnerable claimants, such as those with work-limiting health conditions, or lacking in employment opportunities.

(d)   The Government's commitment that people will always be better off in work should be paramount before applying a sanction for failure to take a job.

(e)   Robust evaluation of the new approach is essential.

6.2. Respondents commented specifically on a number of the Universal Credit regulations and put forward recommendations to ensure that the policy intent is clear, the systems are fair and proportionate, and vulnerable claimants are protected.

The link between the claimant commitment and sanctions

6.3. Respondents noted that the claimant commitment marks a new social contract in which the Government provides work incentives in return for increased conditionality. Several commented that it is vital that the claimant commitment is fully personalised to each claimant's circumstances and that expectations of the claimant are reasonable and fair.

6.4. A number of respondents argued that the claimant commitment should be a two-way commitment which should include a charter of claimants' rights, promoting equal responsibility on both parties: the claimant commitment should set out the support that a claimant can expect to receive as well as their responsibilities.

6.5. Concern was expressed about the wording that the claimant commitment *'must be accepted'* by the claimant, preferring that it *'must be agreed'* by the claimant: this subtle difference would indicate that the claimant has understood the requirements and the penalties that may be applied if they do not comply with them without a good reason. Some respondents proposed that vulnerable clients should be entitled to agree their claimant commitment during a face to face meeting with the advisor.

6.6. Organisations such as the Royal National Institute of Blind People (RNIB) drew attention to the particular barriers faced by partially sighted and blind claimants, arguing that their access needs should be at the heart of any claimant commitment, and that regulations need to reflect the variety of good reasons why they and other people with a disability might fail to comply with it: one suggestion was that failure to comply should automatically trigger an assessment as to whether the conditions in the claimant commitment are reasonable and achievable, in discussion with the claimant, before any sanction is imposed.

Blind and partially sighted people often tell RNIB they receive information from Jobcentre Plus and other public bodies in formats they cannot read. Research shows that inaccessible job adverts represent one of blind and partially sighted people's main barriers to searching for and obtaining employment. Blind and partially sighted individuals' access needs need to be at the heart of any claimant commitment and the regulations need to reflect there are a variety of good reasons why disabled adults might fail to comply with the claimant commitment, not least the provision of inaccessible information or the failure on the part of Jobcentre Plus or other relevant agencies to make reasonable adjustments.

Royal National Institute of Blind People
(submission to SSAC consultation, August 2012)

6.7.   Most respondents believed that the requirement to spend 35 hours a week in job search activities is unhelpful and unenforceable: what is important is that the activities are effective, reflecting quality not quantity of approaches to seeking work. Respondents proposed that the regulation should be reframed around the expectation that the claimant will take all reasonable steps to look for and prepare for work, as agreed in the claimant commitment. Others suggested that it should note any reasons why a claimant may not be able to take up paid work immediately (because they have to find child care, for example, or make arrangements for transport to the place of employment).

6.8. Many respondents argued for flexibility in the conditionality built into the claimant commitment; that exceptions should apply to claimants in specific circumstances; and that conditionality should be lifted, for example when the claimant is sick, such that benefit rules reflect employment rules as far as possible. The lifting of requirements for no more than two periods of two weeks in any one year is regarded as overly restrictive.

Recommendation 23: **The Committee recommends that detailed guidance should be directed towards ensuring that claimant commitment conditions are personalised for each claimant and are reasonable and achievable, taking all the claimant's circumstances into account.**

Imposing sanctions

6.9. There is general consensus that conditionality levels must reflect individual circumstances and that people should not be punished for failures of compliance with conditions that are unreasonable. Respondents drew attention to the following issues:

(a) Ensuring that claimants will be better off in work should be reflected in the sanctions regime: some respondents suggested that, if taking a job would not result in the claimant being better off, this should constitute good reason for failing to apply for or take the job. This could be tested by undertaking a better-off calculation, taking account of work-related expenses including transport and child care, before a sanction is considered.

(b) The regulations provide little incentive for individuals who have been sanctioned to re-engage with their claimant commitment: under the proposed system a sanction would be terminated only after the claimant has been in paid work continuously for six months. Respondents urged that regulation 108(b) should be amended to allow a sanction to be suspended the moment a person enters paid work and terminated completely once the person has been in paid employment for six months, thus ensuring that there is an incentive to take work.

(c) The dual penalty for lower level sanctions might also act as a disincentive to comply with a condition because of the seven day addition: as these sanctions are likely to be applied to the most vulnerable claimants, a system which works instantly to reward engagement is likely to be more effective than one which continues to apply a penalty.

(d) The regulations should make it clear that a claimant will never receive a sanction that exceeds 100 per cent of the Universal Credit standard allowance.

6.10. Organisations working with especially vulnerable claimants commented on the potential negative impacts of a sanction that reduces the amount of the benefit: claimants may fall into arrears with their rent and risk eviction, for example. They suggested that there should be the possibility of automatically triggering direct payment of the housing element of Universal Credit to the claimant's landlord, thus applying a safety net to protect against homelessness.

6.11. Some respondents argued that when considering whether to apply a sanction to a claimant who has voluntarily left employment, assessing whether the claimant acted responsibly is essential. Others have suggested that people may not know whether they are capable of doing a specific job until they have tried it, and the threat of a having a sanction imposed if they leave a job if they subsequently find that the work is not something they can do, should not deter them from trying something new in the first place.

6.12. The limit of five days to provide good reason for failing to comply with a requirement was considered to be too restrictive: before any sanction is imposed a letter, email or text message should be sent to the claimant warning that a sanction is imminent if they do not provide an explanation of the failure. Fears were expressed that vulnerable claimants could find themselves being repeatedly sanctioned for failure to co-operate if there is no statutory duty to contact and interview people who repeatedly fail to meet their conditionality requirements. Specialised support and advice might be needed and referrals should be made to appropriate agencies.

6.13. Several responses raised concerns that sanctions may have negative impacts on children's well being, arguing for sanctions not to be applied to lone parents, for example, without taking children's well being into account. One respondent asked that the local authority be informed when a sanction is applied, and others called for increased support to be available for young people who find it difficult to meet conditionality requirements, urging closer collaboration with charitable sector agencies.

6.14. The higher level sanction of three years drew a lot of comments from, and raised concern amongst, most respondents: such a severe penalty could, they fear, result in claimants turning to the black economy, crime or prostitution; would not incentivise someone to enter employment and would almost certainly damage children growing up in a family where income is severely reduced for a prolonged period. Research[10] from the USA was cited as evidence that severe conditionality can result in families becoming disconnected from society: they are neither in work nor receiving state support. Given the Government's focus on supporting families with children in their early years, respondents urged that this level of sanction should be used with extreme caution.

---

[10] Blank RH and Kovak K. (2008) *Helping Disconnected Single Mothers* National Poverty Center, University of Michigan

6.15. The Committee is sympathetic to the concern expressed by respondents that if sanctions are to be effective in encouraging compliance, continuing a sanction beyond the point of re-engagement may well be counter-productive.

Recommendation 24: The Committee recommends that the Government give consideration to the proposal that a sanction should be suspended when a claimant re-engages and terminated completely only after the claimant has been in work for a period of six months. The sanction could be re-instated if the claimant breaches their conditionality in that period.

In-work sanctions

6.16. A number of comments have been received about how the sanctions regime is to be applied to claimants in work and on low incomes. It is suggested that Universal Credit regulations 80 and 86-87 introduce new complexity into the system. Two requirements appear to cause the most concern here:

(a)   There appears to be an anomaly in Universal Credit regulation 86 which focuses on the steps a claimant must take to obtain paid work. It seems to assume that the claimant is not in any paid work: therefore a claimant who is in work would not appear to meet the letter of this requirement if they took steps to gain skills and increase their earnings potential in the job they currently have, or to overcome other barriers which might be stopping them from increasing their working hours.

(b) The requirement on claimants to be available with 48 hours notice for other job interviews may lead to some employers being less willing to offer part time jobs to Universal Credit claimants if they consider (correctly or not) that the claimant must juggle work search requirements and attend for interviews at short notice, for example.

6.17. Respondents recognised the need for reasonable requirements to be placed on claimants with low earnings to take steps to improve their situation and recommended that this would be better done through a separate, designated regulation with greater emphasis on increasing earnings and greater flexibility in the application of conditionality so as to avoid the risk of unintended consequences. In-work conditionality should be defined and regulated separately from full work search/work availability requirements.

6.18. In-work conditionality is clearly different to the kinds of conditions that will be placed on claimants who are out of work.

Recommendation 25: The Committee suggests that a separate regulation that deals with claimants who are in work would provide clarification of this difference. Moreover, we believe that a staged approach to developing in-work conditionality which is evidence based could ensure that the risk of negative impacts is minimised.

Hardship payments

6.19. A number of respondents referred to the regime for providing hardship payments, noting with some concern that hardship payments are based on need and that they are recoverable. They argued that hardship payments should be easy to access and easy for people to understand.

6.20. One of the main concerns is the introduction of conditionality into the hardship offer: Universal Credit regulation 109 seems to imply that people will have to have met all the work-related requirements within the compliance period. Respondents expressed opposition to this requirement, arguing that hardship payments should act as a safety net to prevent families becoming destitute and to ensure that children have a minimum standard of living. In their response, Barnardo's argued that if this policy continues, there should be a requirement placed on statutory children's services to ensure that safety nets are in place to safeguard children: and a referral should be made to social services when a hardship payment is refused. Furthermore, Barnardo's suggested that Universal Credit regulation 109 (1) (g) should be removed so that even when parents refuse to engage hardship payments are made for the children. This is a model on which the Government may wish to reflect further.

This effectively introduces conditionality into the hardship regime and is something Barnardo's strongly opposes. Hardship payments ought to operate as a safety net to prevent families from entering destitution and ensure that children are provided with a minimum standard of living even when their parents refuse to engage with the system – imposing conditions on families could seriously risk the welfare of children.

If the Government continues with this policy we would urge that all statutory services concerned with the protection of children are required to ensure safety nets are put in place to safeguard the welfare of children. It is particularly important that referrals are made to social services when a hardship payment is refused on the grounds of a failure to engage to ensure the welfare of children is safeguarded. This should ensure that children's welfare is not put at risk by this policy which seeks to remove an important safety net.

Barnardo's
(submission to SSAC consultation, August 2012)

6.21. Respondents were of the view that making hardship payments recoverable means that claimants subject to a sanction would continue to receive a reduced rate of Universal Credit for months after the sanction has terminated. This could, they fear, lead to increased debt and continuing hardship for long periods of time.

Evaluation

6.22. Respondents highlighted the importance of comprehensive evaluation of the new conditionality and sanctions regimes and the flexibility to make changes based on the early evidence. The evaluation needs to:

- measure the impact of encouraging people in to work;
- examine the extent to which the claimant commitment is tailored to individual needs and is achievable;
- measure the deterrent effect of conditionality and sanctions;
- monitor who is sanctioned and the reasons given;
- measure the impact of each level of sanctioning on individuals and families;
- consider the training and skills required by personal advisors and decision makers to make the new arrangements effective, transparent and fair;
- determine any unintended consequences;
- examine the hardship arrangements and the extent to which they act as a safety net;
- consider the extent to which the conditionality requirements and the sanctions imposed are proportionate; and
- monitor the impacts on and outcomes for specific groups including people with mental health problems and/or learning disabilities, and people whose first language is not English.

Recommendation 26: The Committee endorses the need for robust and comprehensive evaluation of the new sanction arrangements and is keen to assist in the design and development of this.

7. Claims and payments

7.1. The proposed claims and payments regulation are designed to provide the legislative framework for claiming and paying:

- Universal Credit;
- Personal Independence Payment (PIP);
- Employment and Support Allowance (ESA); and
- Jobseeker's Allowance (JSA).

7.2. Universal Credit and PIP are new benefits, provision for which is made in the Welfare Reform Act 2012. ESA and JSA, in the context of the Claims and Payments Regulations 2012, are the contributory elements of both benefits.

On-line accessibility

7.3. The Department's ambition to make on-line the primary method of claiming Universal Credit has generated a significant response from a diverse group of individuals and organisations. There is widespread recognition of the economic and administrative advantages of an effective on-line system, both for government and for individuals. For example it will:

(a) enable claimants to be well-informed and to manage their claims in their own homes; and

(b) enable the claim process to be flexible, simple and efficient. For example claimants will be able to make claims at a time that suits them, will not have to read through material irrelevant to their circumstances, and will be prompted to complete all of the relevant fields on the form thereby minimising the risk of defective claims being submitted to the Department.

7.4.   However, a number of concerns were raised about the degree to which a lack of access could lead to the exclusion of those individuals and businesses that currently do not have access to broadband facilities in a private and secure environment or do not have the necessary skills to complete and maintain a claim on-line. These are outlined in more detail below.

Access

7.5.   A number of respondents noted that a significant minority of claimants do not have access to a computer at home and will have to rely on libraries, welfare rights organisations, internet cafés or family or friends to provide the necessary means to make a claim. This assertion is underpinned by recent research[11] commissioned by DWP which shows that 30 per cent of people likely to be eligible for Universal Credit do not have a computer in their home; and that 22 per cent have never used the internet (with a further 30 per cent being only occasional users).

7.6.   Respondents also highlighted a number of potential concerns about the use of computers outside the home to make a benefit claim. For example:

(a)   *Demand*: some welfare rights organisations reported that the demand on the computers made available in their offices for job search activity was already high, and were concerned that this would be further exacerbated by the shift to on-line claiming. We note, however, that the Department has already recognised this as a potential difficulty. Indeed, during their recent visit to Streatham Jobcentre, Committee members observed that arrangements had been put in place to procure twelve new computers for claimants to use for making and maintaining claims to Universal Credit.

---

[11] Tu, T. and Ginnis, S. (2012) *Work and the welfare system: a survey of benefits and tax credit recipients*

(b)   *Accessibility*: some respondents considered this to be a particular challenge for disabled people who might require specialist IT equipment (which is unlikely to be readily available on public computers) to facilitate accessibility, and for those living in rural areas who might have to travel some distance (and incur high travel costs) to the nearest library or internet café to make the initial claim and subsequently maintain it. A number of submissions also drew attention to the poor broadband coverage in some parts of the country, particularly in rural areas, both for claimants and for their employers. This was, in particular, a concern for farmers who would be required to use the internet to meet their monthly reporting requirements.

(c)   *Security and privacy:*   respondents described the security and privacy of on-line claims as a major concern among people likely to be eligible for Universal Credit, especially for people using a public access computer to make their claim – and particularly so if they are novice users.

Nearly half of those seeking help on tax and tax credit issues do not have access to a computer...

...strategy should take into account accessibility of computers and internet connections for low-income households. It is sometimes suggested that public computers in libraries or internet cafes are generally available, but at a cost in terms of security and increased incidence of fraud and error. People carrying out financial transactions on public computers are more vulnerable to being watched by strangers, or if they fail to close and log out of a session completely they leave themselves open to fraud.

Low Income Tax Reform Group
(submission to SSAC consultation, August 2012)

> *… unclear how third parties such as CAB advisers will be able to provide support for claimants without first having to support them to access their bank accounts, which will involve the use of personal data and passwords etc.*
>
> **Citizen's Advice Bureau**
> **(submission to SSAC consultation, August 2012)**

Skills

7.7. A number of respondents raised concerns about whether all claimants would have the necessary skills and confidence to complete a claim form on-line or to maintain that claim afterwards. They highlighted, in particular, the challenges that this would pose for people with learning disabilities or for whom English is not a first language. Providing both access and practical help to these groups is likely to be a challenge, and respondents from local authorities and third sector organisations noted that they would be unable to take on this role without the provision of additional government funding.

7.8. The Government's stated ambition is for 80 per cent of claims to be made on-line, however the consultation has highlighted some specific challenges for the Department to reflect on further before it is likely to achieve that.

<u>Recommendation 27</u>: The Committee recommends that the Government considers establishing, on the basis of what it has learned from previous attempts to encourage a shift to on-line channels, a phased take-up over a transitional period. The aim should be to optimise the prospects of securing the maximum shift over time to on-line channels consistent with appropriate protection for vulnerable claimants.

Recommendation 28: The Committee urges the Government to ensure that it has sufficient resources in place to support those claimants who are initially unable to make claims on-line because of capability or accessibility difficulties, to make claims by telephone or, where appropriate, through a home visit.

Recommendation 29: Additionally, the content of information leaflets and guidance notes on making a claim on-line should be clear and unambiguous, using language that occasional computer users will readily understand. It should also explain what they should do to make a claim in the event that they are unable to do so on-line having followed that guidance. The Committee would welcome an opportunity to review and comment on drafts of any communications material being produced.

Monthly payments: budgeting

7.9. Universal Credit will be assessed each calendar month, paid monthly in arrears as a single payment and to one person in a couple. The submissions received by the Committee generally focused on the impact that the move to monthly payments would have on household budgets, although there were also a small group of respondents who outlined potential untended consequences that could arise from the introduction of a single payment or making payment to one person.

Monthly payments

7.10. While respondents welcomed the move to monthly payments, they also noted its potential to disrupt the budgeting of those claimants who are normally engaged in weekly paid employment and, consequently, budget weekly.

7.11. The Personal Finance Research Centre advised the Committee that around 28 per cent of all employees are paid weekly, rising to 42 per cent of those in the lowest two income quintiles. A significant proportion of people receiving Universal Credit will, therefore, either already have a weekly income from employment or will just have left a job where they were paid weekly. The explanatory memorandum[12] provided to the Committee acknowledges that the shift in payment frequency has the potential to cause major disruption to household budgets for those families.

When potential UC claimants were asked directly if they would find it harder to budget with monthly payments:

- 42 per cent said that they would find it harder (80 per cent of this group said they were likely to run out of money before the end of the month)
- 10 per cent said that it would be easier
- 40 per cent said that it would make no difference
- 7 percent already received monthly payments

**Work and the welfare system:
a survey of benefits and tax credit recipients**[13]

7.12. Respondents, particularly organisations working with vulnerable claimants (including people with learning difficulties, the homeless, those with a transient lifestyle and those with drug or alcohol dependencies etc) were concerned about the ability of some claimants to manage a monthly budget, and noted that it was their experience that budgeting over short time periods enabled people to keep tighter control of their

---

[12] For the Universal Credit, Personal Independence Payment and Working-age Benefits (Claims and Payments) Regulations 2012
[13] Tu, T. and Ginnis, S. (2012) *Work and the welfare system: a survey of benefits and tax credit recipients*

finances. There was also a view that the intention to pay the PIP four-weekly built in an unnecessary layer of complexity for disabled people.

7.13. In view of the evidence cited above the Committee welcomes the Department's intention to allow some exceptions to monthly payments.

7.14. The Committee also welcomes the Government's intention to provide education on financial management and to offer other professional assistance to support people in moving from weekly to monthly budgets.

Recommendation 30: The Committee looks forward to receiving the detailed proposals for this support and would encourage the Government to monitor its impact to ensure it is effective and responsive to the needs of claimants.

A single payment

7.15. A significant number of responses, including from a wide variety of landlords and their representative bodies, expressed concern about the inclusion of housing costs within the single payment to tenants. They assert that the changes will lead to high levels of rent arrears and eviction of claimants, and bad debt levels for landlords creating an upward pressure on rents.

7.16. Information provided to the Committee during the consultation suggests that a considerable minority of social tenants will be at risk of falling into rent arrears. Should that occur, it would undermine the viability of smaller providers of supported housing. Some providers of supported housing quantified the impact of various levels of rent arrears (from 15 to 50 per cent) on their financial viability.

Recommendation 31: The Committee welcomes the Government's intention to retain direct payment in some circumstances but, since the criteria will be set out in guidance, it would encourage the Government to consult landlords, their representatives and other stakeholders on its provisions. The Committee also looks forward to learning about the results of the social sector demonstration projects and urges the Government to take account of their findings.

Payment to one person

7.17. Respondents broadly welcomed the move to pay Universal Credit to one person, although acknowledged that it would present challenges for a minority of claimants. There was a view that women in particular would be unfairly disadvantaged under this payment model, since men in low-income households are more likely to determine how the household budget is allocated, often giving their wife or partner only sufficient money to cover the essentials. Respondents were especially concerned that payments relating to children in the household would not be paid separately to the main carer.

Joint claims

7.18. Couples will be required to make a joint claim for Universal Credit, with both asked for a 'claimant commitment'. If one of them fails to make that commitment the couple will not be entitled to benefit. A number of respondents highlighted scenarios where joint claims had the potential to be problematic, for example where one partner might be unwilling to sign the claimant commitment.

Recommendation 32: Clear guidance is needed on how such cases should be handled, and whether in a limited number of cases, the claim may be processed for one member of the couple as a single person to avoid hardship.

7.19. A further concern raised by organisations that operate refuges and supported housing was the need to protect the confidentiality of personal details (particularly addresses) submitted by people who have been subject to domestic abuse.

Recommendation 33: Necessary arrangements will need to be put in place to ensure that the safety of these individuals is not compromised.

Date of claim and entitlement, including allowing an earlier date of claim

7.20. There will be three circumstances in which the decision maker may be required to make a back-dating decision on a claim for Universal Credit. These are where a late claim stems from:

- A failure to send the claimant a timely notification of another benefit's expiry.
- Health or disability factors.
- A failure (of maintenance) of the computer system.

7.21. A large number of submissions indicated that they thought this list was too restrictive. In comparison to the current back-dating rules relating to income support and JSA, the proposed Universal Credit rules omit several prescribed circumstances where back-dating of the claim up to one month or three months is permitted. For example, the omissions include the following scenarios:

- Claimants with learning difficulties or who are unable to manage their affairs but have no appointee.
- The death of a close relative or caring commitments.
- A domestic emergency.
- The receipt of misleading benefit advice.

7.22. Respondents argue that these omissions could result in hardship for some claimants, especially as Universal Credit payments are to be made monthly in arrears, and have suggested that the 'good cause' provisions for back dating be retained.

Recommendation 34: The Committee supports the view that 'good cause' provisions for back-dating should be retained in some limited cases, for example where a claimant has received misleading benefit advice, and recommends that the Government reflect further on this point.

Amending, failing to complete and withdrawing a claim

7.23. If a person makes their claim for benefit on-line there is an obvious case for communicating on-line with them once the award is in place. However respondents have noted that this assumes that access to the internet is still readily available and this may not be the case. For example, someone who made their claim using a computer outside their home may not be in a position to check their emails regularly. Therefore it is possible that a claimant could fail to pick up an email asking them to attend a work-focused interview and be sanctioned for failing to comply. Similarly, a claimant may fail to see an email request to provide information to ensure that the current award remains correct leading to a suspension of benefit payments.

Recommendation 35: The Committee would encourage the Government to review its arrangements for communicating with claimants who are less able to maintain their award on-line regularly, for example where they are relying on public access computers. The use of text message alerts or smart phone applications are options that should be explored.

When claimants are paid

7.24. A number of the respondents to our consultation have two concerns in terms of when claimants are paid:

- The long wait - about five and a half weeks - before the first Universal Credit payment is received: concerns were raised about tenants falling into arrears with their rent; using high-cost credit to tide them over this period; or non-payment of other household bills leading to arrears from which it will be difficult to recover.

- The payment date being fixed in relation to the date of the claim: there is a concern that, as many originators of direct debits are inflexible about the date on which payments can be made, a lack of alignment between this and Universal Credit payment dates could lead to budgeting difficulties. Landlords and housing organisations were, in particular, concerned that this could lead to tenants running up arrears on their rent. While landlords could, in theory, tailor the rent due dates for claimants to align them with the Universal Credit payment dates, that would be more complicated and costly for landlords to monitor.

Recommendation 36: The Committee recommends that this is an area on which the Government should reflect further in order to find a solution that accommodates the needs of claimants, the originators of direct debits as well as its own needs for simplicity.

8. Conclusions and recommendations

8.1   As noted earlier in the report, the Government's proposals for simplifying the benefit system have the broad support of a significant number of respondents to the Committee's consultation. The regulations provided by the Department in June had a number of acknowledged gaps on which work was still in progress. Subject to that, and having considered all of the evidence submitted during the consultation, the Committee's conclusion is that, measured against the Government's declared intent, the draft regulations considered within this report have an overall coherence.

8.2   The Committee has, however, drawn attention to some significant and specific concerns in this report. These suggest there may be risks to the delivery of the Government's intent, and that there might also be an unreasonable impact on vulnerable groups of benefit recipients. In some cases the Committee is recommending that the Government reconsider those points before finalising the draft regulations. In others it recognises that, due to current uncertainties, the points are better addressed through monitoring and evaluation during the initial implementation phase.

8.3   The points on which the Committee is making specific recommendations are set out below.

Definitions and guidance

(i)   The Government should ensure that its regulations and underpinning guidance contain clear, consistent and unambiguous definitions. The Committee would welcome an opportunity to comment on the draft guidance to ensure that it achieves this. *[Paragraph 2.5]*

Monitoring and evaluation

(ii)   The Government should establish a robust monitoring mechanism and evaluation process to facilitate rapid and informed responses to emerging issues as Universal Credit is rolled out. The Committee would welcome the opportunity to provide support in shaping and monitoring these evaluation arrangements. *[Paragraph 2.7]*

IT development

(iii)   The Government should consider carefully the impact of any amendments to the Universal Credit regulations on the IT delivery plans, particularly in terms of available resources and the potential for delay and errors. In particular, the Committee would be concerned if a significant number of additional manual processing steps were to be introduced in order to accommodate changes to the regulations, and would encourage the Government to consider carefully how and when the full implementation is best phased in to permit the optimum application of the new IT system. *[Paragraph 2.8]*

Self employed

(iv)   The Government should engage further with self employed organisations and their service providers on their concerns about monthly reporting in order to identify how the concerns raised might be resolved. For example, there would be merit in exploring the degree to which quarterly reporting, with a requirement to submit the necessary records within 15 days of the end of that period, would work within the Universal Credit regime. *[Paragraphs 3.6]*

(v)   The Government should give further consideration to a full reconciliation being undertaken at the end of the final quarter when gains and losses are properly balanced out and aligned with self assessment returns being submitted to HMRC. *[Paragraph 3.6]*

(vi)   Given the concerns raised about the practicalities of the monthly reporting arrangements, the Government should consider piloting the arrangements with a sufficient number of self employed people to be truly representative before introducing any new arrangements in 2014. *[Paragraph 3.6]*

(vii)   The inability to roll forward losses from an earlier assessment period is likely to disadvantage unfairly those self employed individuals and small businesses whose income flows are irregular and/or seasonal. The Committee recommends that this is looked at again. *[Paragraph 3.11]*

(viii)   The Government should reflect further on the list of exclusions from permitted expenses (for example, expenses 'incurred unreasonably', expenditure on cars, and interest payments). *[Paragraph 3.12]*

(ix)   DWP and HMRC should move towards a unified reporting regime (with the timescales for implementation harmonised) that will both assist compliance and keep administrative burdens on small and 'start up' businesses to a minimum. *[Paragraph 3.17]*

(x)   The Government should allow claimants more than one start-up period in a lifetime. The Prince's Trust has proposed that there should be a specified minimum period - say, three years - which must elapse before a further start-up period would be allowed. Given their considerable experience of supporting young people in establishing businesses, this suggestion should be explored further. *[Paragraph 3.22]*

(xi)   The Government should give further consideration to the impact on industry groups likely to be disproportionately affected by the Universal Credit regulations, and to engage with them on developing innovative ways in which their concerns might be overcome. *[Paragraph 3.25]*

(xii)   Given the potential impact of quasi self employment on vulnerable claimants, the Government should provide further clarity on the responsibilities of the Government, employers and their intermediaries, and individual jobseekers in determining the employment status of posts, in particular for the purpose of reporting income. *[Paragraph 3.28]*

(xiii)   The Government should consider carefully the formal guidance that will be applied to the application of conditionality and the minimum income floor in cases where a claimant, while technically self-employed, is in fact in a situation of seeking work rather than developing a business. This will safeguard against those who are not developing a business being inadvertently treated by the Department as if they are. *[Paragraph 3.28]*

(xiv)   Immediately prior to, and during the early implementation of, Universal Credit for the self employed, a level of discretion and system flexibility should be maintained to allow initial learning to be reflected in its application and thus avoid it being discredited by unintended outcomes. *[Paragraph 3.30]*

Housing

(xv)   Given the inevitable tension between the position of landlords and tenants in terms of direct payments, and as only limited evidence is available about the likely behavioural impacts of the change, the Committee recommends that this is a particularly important area that the Government should keep under review, in particular by putting in place arrangements for effective monitoring and evaluation. *[Paragraph 4.5]*

(xvi)   The Government should clarify the wording *'services necessary to maintain the fabric of the dwelling'* in the regulations. *[Paragraph 4.11]*

(xvii)   Given the volume of responses received commenting on service charges, and the very wide variation in the potential impact described within them, it is not easy to identify where the eligibility line might most sensibly be drawn. However it is a clear area of concern for many and the Committee would urge the Government to engage quickly with key stakeholders, some of whom have acknowledged the need to simplify and streamline the existing rules, to discuss further whether the policy intention and practical consequences are sufficiently understood and aligned. *[Paragraph 4.11]*

(xviii)   The Government should reflect further on the potential consequences of the under-occupancy proposals on the recently bereaved, disabled children and adults (including those with behavioural issues and overnight care needs); and on family members who are temporarily absent from the family home but where there is clear evidence that they will rejoin the family unit at some point in the near future. *[Paragraph 4.12]*

(xix)   As a significant number of responses called for the provision of accommodation for those that need intensive and often specialised care and support to be taken out of the Universal Credit system, the Government should reflect on those concerns further in reaching detailed decisions on this sensitive area of policy. *[Paragraph 4.13]*

(xx)   The Government should put arrangements in place to monitor and evaluate the impact of the Support for Mortgage Interest 'zero earnings rule'. *[Paragraph 4.15]*

(xxi)   The Government should give further consideration to the issues that have been raised regarding the impact of the proposals on refuges for people fleeing the fear of violence, and engage directly with key stakeholders on the issue. *[Paragraph 4.17]*

Benefit Cap

(xxii)   The Government should, in close co-operation with local authorities, undertake a robust monitoring and evaluation programme along the lines outlined in section 5 of this report, and to use it to inform any appropriate adjustments to the implementation of the overall benefits cap policy. In evaluating the effectiveness of this policy, the totality of costs to the taxpayer (whether through central or local government) should be considered rather than monitoring savings delivered to the Department's benefit expenditure in isolation. *[Paragraph 5.8]*

Sanctions

(xxiii)   The Government should ensure that detailed guidance is directed towards ensuring that claimant commitment conditions are personalised for each claimant and are reasonable and achievable, taking all the claimant's circumstances into account. *[Paragraph 6.8]*

(xxiv)   The Government should give consideration to the proposal that a sanction should be suspended when a claimant re-engages and terminated completely only after the claimant has been in work for a period of six months. The sanction could be re-instated if the claimant breaches their conditionality in that period. *[Paragraph 6.15]*

(xxv)   In-work conditionality is clearly different to the kinds of conditions that will be placed on claimants that are out of work. The Government should consider introducing a separate regulation that deals with claimants who are in work to provide clarification of this difference. It should also consider a staged approach to developing in-work conditionality which is evidence based to ensure that the risk of negative impacts is minimised. *[Paragraph 6.18]*

(xxvi) The Government should undertake robust and comprehensive evaluation of the new sanction arrangements. The Committee is keen to assist in the design and development of this. *[Paragraph 6.22]*

Claims and Payments

(xxvii) The Government should consider establishing, on the basis of what it has learned from previous attempts to encourage a shift to on-line channels, a phased take-up over a transitional period. The aim should be to optimise the prospects of securing the maximum shift over time to on-line channels consistent with appropriate protection for vulnerable claimants. *[Paragraph 7.8]*

(xxviii) The Government should ensure that it has sufficient resources in place to support those claimants who are initially unable to make claims on-line because of capability or accessibility difficulties, to make claims by telephone or, where appropriate, through a home visit. *[Paragraph 7.8]*

(xxix) The content of information leaflets and guidance notes on making a claim on-line should be clear and unambiguous, using language that occasional computer users will readily understand. It should also explain what they should do to make a claim in the event that they are unable to do so on-line having followed that guidance. The Committee would welcome an opportunity to review and comment on drafts of any communications material being produced. *[Paragraph 7.8]*

(xxx) The Committee looks forward to receiving detailed proposals for the provision of education on financial management and the provision of other professional assistance to support people in moving from weekly to monthly budgets. It recommends that the Government should monitor the impact of this support to ensure that it is effective and responsive to the needs of claimants. *[Paragraph 7.14]*

(xxxi) The Committee welcomes the Government's intention to retain direct payment in some circumstances but, since the criteria will be set out in guidance, it would encourage the Government to consult landlords, their representatives and other stakeholders on its provisions. The Committee also looks forward to learning about the results of the social sector demonstration projects and urges the Department to take account of their findings. *[Paragraph 7.16]*

(xxxii) Clear guidance will be required on handling 'joint claims' where one member of a couple fails to make a 'claimant commitment'. The Government should also consider whether, in a limited number of cases, the claim may be processed for one member of the couple as a single person to avoid hardship. *[Paragraph 7.18]*

(xxxiii) The Government should ensure that the necessary arrangements are put in place to safeguard the confidentiality of personal details (particularly addresses) submitted by people who have been subject to domestic abuse. *[Paragraph 7.19]*

(xxxiv) The Government should retain 'good cause' provisions for back-dating in some limited cases, for example where a claimant has received misleading benefit advice. *[Paragraph 7.22]*

(xxxv) The Government should review its arrangements for communicating with those claimants who are less able to maintain their award on-line regularly, for example where they are relying on public access computers. The use of text message alerts or smart phone applications are options that should be explored. *[Paragraph 7.23]*

(xxxvi) The Government should reflect further on when payments are made in order to find a solution that accommodates the needs of claimants, the originators of direct debits, as well as its own needs for simplicity. *[Paragraph 7.24]*

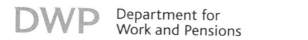 Department for
Work and Pensions

Universal Credit Policy Division

Our address   3rd Floor
Caxton House
6-12 Tothill Street
London
SW1H 9NA

Denise Whitehead
Committee Secretary
Social Security Advisory Committee
The Adelphi
1-11 John Adam Street
London.
WC2N 6HT

3rd August 2012

Dear Denise,

UNIVERSAL CREDIT REGULATIONS

We have been continuing to work on the package of draft Universal Credit regulations that were referred to the Committee in June. We are now in a position to provide some more detail for the Committee and the reasons why we think some changes are needed.

The annexes attached to this note set out the areas in which we have refined our thinking, broken down by regulation.

I would ask the Committee to note these changes.

Officials will be happy to answer any questions about these changes.

Charlotte Wightwick

Deputy Director, Universal Credit Policy Division

Claims and Payments Regulations

1. On claims to Universal Credit by joint claimants, the draft regulations (CP10) state currently that when a benefit unit separates the decision about which member will be able to maintain their entitlement without having to make a new claim will be made by the Secretary of State. We now wish to provide that it is the couple themselves who will make the decision about which of them is to maintain the Universal Credit claim without having to reclaim, and which member will make a new claim. The Secretary of State will only decide if the couple cannot reach a decision.

2. On JSA claims, we are omitting regulation CP18(6) which treated the first day of claiming JSA online as the date of claim provided a claim was submitted within 7 days. Its removal results in equality of treatment between JSA and Universal Credit online claimants and simplifies the development of supporting IT systems.

3. On childcare, we propose to clarify regulations on evidence and information in connection with an award. The policy intention is to be able to contact a childcare provider to request information in connection with childcare costs claimed in Universal Credit. The draft regulations (CP 36(7) allow the Secretary Of State to request information and evidence from a childcare provider in connection with a claim for childcare costs in Universal Credit. We also need a similar provision to request information and evidence from a childcare provider in connection with an ongoing award for childcare costs. We would use this provision to verify for instance that the child is with that childcare provider, the days/hours of attendance and costs. The change will deliver the policy intent.

4. We are proposing changes to regulation CP22(3)(a) to clarify which benefits the phrase "another benefit" refers to by listing the benefits, i.e. JSA, ESA, IS, Working Tax Credit and Child Tax Credit. We are also making equivalent changes to regulation CP25(5)(d) in respect of a jobseeker's allowance.

5. We have also clarified regulation CP30(1)(c) and added in a new paragraph (d) to clarify that the date of notification of intention to make a claim by telephone will only be preserved as the date of claim where DWP staff are unable to accept the claim on that day, e.g. due to lack of resources, not where the claimant is unable to make the claim on that day.

6. We have included a new provision at regulation CP44(7) which provides for a daily rate of benefit to be calculated. Unfortunately due to an oversight this provision was not included in the draft seen by SSAC members at the meeting on 13/14 June 2012. This regulation provides the formula to calculate a part month payment of Universal Credit. At present we would need to do this when a Universal Credit claimant reaches the qualifying age for State Pension Credit part way through their assessment period as we

intend to pay Universal Credit to reflect the number of days they were eligible for Universal Credit.

7. We are making a minor clarification to Schedule 5 of the Claims and Payments Regulations to the effect that deductions in respect of eligible loan recovery may be made from contributory benefits in cases where Universal Credit is not in payment, as well as in cases where there is insufficient Universal Credit in payment to take the full deduction. This clarification corrects an omission in the earlier draft regulations and carries forward existing policy.

8. We propose to clarify the interpretation regulations to remove the definition of "claim for benefit". This definition is not required. In existing benefits this is intended to cover adult dependency increases and child dependency increases where a separate claim is needed for the increase to be applied. The addition of a child or partner to a Universal Credit award is a change of circumstances requiring a supersession decision rather than a separate claim.

9. The draft claims and payments regulations set out what should happen if more than one person is liable to pay maintenance in a polygamous marriage, which has been brought forward from the current Claims and Payments Regulations. However, as polygamous marriages will not be recognised in Universal Credit, the inclusion of this regulation was an oversight and is not needed.

10. On Disability Living Allowance and Personal Independence Payments, Section.82 of the Welfare Reform Act 2012 provides for claims to be made where the claimant is terminally ill (as defined) either by the claimant or by a third party, with or without the claimant's knowledge. We are proposing changes to CP31 to protect the original date of claim where a claim has been received by a third party and the Secretary of State determines that the claimant is not terminally ill. The provision would act in a similar way to that at CP31(3) and is designed to work in the best interests of the claimant. This change carries on what we do in Disability Living Allowance (DLA) where we will be seeking to clarify the existing Claims and Payments Regulations 1987 to put this process on a firmer and more explicit legislative basis.

11. We are making clear in regulation CP55(3) that Personal Independence Payment is a benefit paid solely for the benefit of the claimant, rather than a benefit for the household, by deleting the words "or any other person".

12. We have corrected an oversight that brought through wholesale to CP56 provisions currently at Regulation 42 of the Claims and Payments Regulations 1987. We did not carry forward powers from the Contributions and Benefits Act 1992 to the Welfare Reform Act 2012 to not allow payment of the mobility component of Personal Independence Payment where the person has the use of an invalid carriage or other vehicle provided by the NHS. The provisions for DLA principally linked with the provisions of the old

invalid vehicle scheme (the blue "trikes") and were designed to encourage users to relinquish their vehicle in favour of either cash receipt through the mobility component of DLA or a motor car or powered wheelchair where payment of the mobility component was transferred to the Motability scheme. We are satisfied that there are either no such "trikes" or their use is so limited that the continued provisions for Personal Independence Payment were unnecessary. We are also satisfied that provision of powered wheelchairs by the NHS provides complementary provision to that enabled through the Motability scheme, rather than overlapping provision.

Decision Making and Appeals Regulations

13. Following the policy change outlined in paragraph 1 above, if a couple do not decide who will maintain the claim and the Secretary of State has to step in as a last resort to decide, the decision of the Secretary of State to shall not be appealable.

14. On overpayments, paragraph 14(d) to (f) of Schedule 4 to the draft Decision and Appeals Regulations could never apply to a PIP overpayment, so we propose to omit them.

15. In relation to paragraph 16 of that Schedule, the long-standing policy is that all short-term advances are recoverable (whether overpaid or not) so we plan to omit sub-paragraph (a) of that paragraph.

16. Off-setting of short-term advances is covered in paragraph 15 of Schedule 4, so we propose to omit paragraph 16 (e).

17. In terms of the list of exceptions to the general position in paragraph 16 of Schedule 4 that decisions under Social Security (Recovery of Benefit) Regulations 2012 do not carry appeal rights, we are proposing to add decisions under regulation 9 (sums to be deducted: change of dwelling) to that list. Such decisions will, therefore, carry the right of appeal.

Jobseekers Allowance Regulations

18. In line with the assurances given to SSAC in June, we have been examining the detail of the draft JSA regulations to ensure that, for example, definitions are as consistent as possible with other benefits. As a consequence of that work, we have established that additional provisions are required within the regulations to maintain the current policy on treatment of students. At present, most students are excluded from JSA because, under Regulation 15 of the current regulations, they are regarded as not available for employment.

19. This provision was not carried forward into the draft regulations presented to SSAC and we are currently considering how best to maintain the current policy. This does not affect the principle in our memorandum to SSAC that, with the exception of labour market conditionality and sanctions provisions, we are intending to retain all of the key features of contributory JSA.

20. We have also noted that we have not carried forward notional earnings provisions to the new JSA Regulations. Although these provisions are only rarely used, they currently apply to contributory JSA as well as to income-based JSA. We therefore intend to remedy the omission.

21. We are clarifying the JSA regulations to carry forward easements to availability and earnings rules for reserve forces attending annual training. These changes are being introduced for the current regulations by the JSA (Members of the Forces) Regulations which were presented to SSAC in April and come into force on 30 July.

Conditionality and sanctions provisions applying to the Jobseeker's Allowance, Employment and Support Allowance and Universal Credit Regulations

22. We intend to make a number of changes to the conditionality and sanctions provisions. These will involve changes to all three sets of regulations for JSA, ESA and UC. In addition, they are being redrafted more generally so they are simpler and easier to understand.

23. We will use a formula to calculate the amount of a sanction. The UC Regulations referred to SSAC had a space holder to express the sanction amount and the ESA and JSA Regulations set out actual sanction amounts. We are proposing that this is replaced by a formula to calculate the sanction amount in line with the updated standard allowance (for UC) and uprated age related allowance (for JSA and ESA) every year. This approach will therefore negate the need to up -rate actual sanction amounts in regulations. Sanctions will continue to be equivalent to the claimant's standard allowance for UC and their age related allowance for JSA and ESA. These changes apply to the UC, ESA and JSA regulations.

24. We will be clarifying that the time limit for accepting the claimant commitment can be extended to allow for a "cooling off period" and also where the person has objected and the Secretary of State considered that the objection is justified. Where the time limit set by the Secretary of State has not been met, then the claimant has failed to satisfy a condition of entitlement. The Secretary of State can either disallow that claim or can start the award from the date when condition is met. The effect is that a person will receive benefit from the date of claim provided they accept the claimant commitment in the time that the Secretary of State sets. These changes apply to the UC, ESA and JSA regulations.

25. On the 'No Escalation' rule, the Explanatory Memoranda sent to SSAC noted that if a claimant commits multiple failures within the same compliance period (which we expected to be a two weekly period) then the sanction would not escalate to the next level. This rule will help to ensure that claimants do not accumulate lengthy sanctions in a short period of time. We have now confirmed that sanctions will not escalate if a claimant commits more than one failure within the same two week period – so for

example, if a claimant commits a high level failure in Week 1 and receives a 91 day sanction and then commits a further high level failure in Week 2 then the second sanction he will receive will be 91 days rather than 182 days sanction. These changes apply to the UC, ESA and JSA regulations

26. On the effective date of sanctions, the changes below apply to the JSA and ESA regulations only.

27. On JSA, the Explanatory Memorandum sent to SSAC noted that where the Secretary of State has determined that a sanction will apply it will take effect from the first day of the benefit week in which the failure occurred unless the claimant has already been paid for that period at the time the decision to sanction is made, in which case the sanction is to be applied from the first day of the benefit week after the one for which the claimant was last paid JSA.

28. Regulation 20 made slightly different provision. It noted that the reduction should take effect from:

    a)   the first day of the benefit week in which the failure occurred,

    b)   where the payment of a jobseeker's allowance for the benefit week referred to in paragraph (a) is not reduced in accordance with the Secretary of State's determination, the first day of the next benefit week,

    c)   where the amount of the award of the jobseeker's allowance for the benefit week referred to in paragraph (a) or (b) is already subject to a reduction because of a determination under section 6J or 6K of the Act, the first day in respect of which the amount of the award is no longer subject to a reduction

29. We intend to clarify the regulation to ensure that the sanction is taken from:
    a)   where a jobseeker's allowance <u>has not</u> been paid for the benefit week in which the failure occurred, the first day of that benefit week;

    b)   where a jobseeker's allowance <u>has</u> been paid for the benefit week in which the failure occurred, the first day of the first benefit week for which a jobseeker's allowance has not been paid (this will help to avoid an overpayment, for example, where a sanction is not input to the system in time); or

    c)   where the award is already subject to a reduction then the first day of the benefit week in which the award is no longer subject to a reduction.

30. On ESA, the Explanatory Memorandum sent to SSAC noted that where the Secretary of State has determined that a sanction will apply it will take effect from the first day of the benefit week in which that determination is made (or the following week if a payment has already been released).

31. Regulation 52 made slightly different provision, it noted that the reduction should take effect from:

a) the first day of the benefit week in which the failure occurred,

b) where the payment of an employment and support allowance for the benefit week referred to in paragraph (a) is not reduced in accordance with the Secretary of State's determination, the first day of the next benefit week,

c) where the amount of the award of the employment and support allowance for the benefit week referred to in paragraph (a) or (b) is already subject to a reduction because of a determination under section 11J of the Act, the first day in respect of which the amount of the award is no longer subject to a reduction.

32. We intend to clarify the regulation to ensure that the sanction is taken from:

a) where employment and support allowance has not been paid for the benefit week in which the determination is made, the first day of that benefit week;

b) where an employment and support allowance has been paid for the benefit week in which the determination is made, the first day of the first benefit week for which an employment and support allowance has not been paid (this will help to avoid an overpayment, for example, where a sanction is not input to the system in time); or

c) where the award is already subject to a reduction then the first day of the benefit week in which the award is no longer subject to a reduction.

33. We are taking different approaches for effective dates for JSA and ESA. For JSA where a jobseeker's allowance has not been paid for the benefit week in which the failure occurred, the reduction will apply from the first day of that benefit week. For ESA where an employment and support allowance has not been paid for the benefit week in which the determination occurred, the reduction will apply from the first day of that benefit week.

34. A different approach is being taken for ESA because payments are issued automatically in advance of the claimant's payday and if we used the JSA approach whereby the reduction will take effect from the first day of the benefit week in which the failure occurred, there would be an increased risk of overpayments occurring.

Universal Credit Main Scheme Regulations

1. On housing, new provisions will exclude the liability to pay rent where the payments are to a trust where a trustee or beneficiary is a member of the assessment unit or a close relative who lives in the same property.

2. We have simplified the rules so that housing costs can be paid indefinitely where rent is waived because the tenant is undertaking repair/renovation work on their accommodation.

3. Non-dependent couples are to be treated as individuals, so changes are to be made to ensure they are each allocated a room and each pays the housing cost contribution unless exempt. Changes will be made to remove references to both members of a couple having to meet the criteria before an exemption applies. In addition reference to a lone parent with a child under 5 will be changed to a person responsible for a child under 5.

4. The shared accommodation rate is to apply only to claimants who are single, childless and aged under 35, unless exempt. The SAR will be automatic for this group so a definition of shared accommodation is unnecessary and will be removed.

5. The under-occupancy calculation will not be undertaken for joint tenants living in the social rented sector receiving Universal Credit.

6. We are making a clarificatory change to ensure that current housing costs can continue be met indefinitely whilst repairs are being carried out on the claimants home.

7. In contrived liability cases we will refer not only to instances where the contrivance has been made in order to secure the inclusion of the housing costs element but also refer to increasing the amount of the housing costs element.

8. We have corrected errors that became apparent in the regulations in relation to close relatives, companies and trusts. The reference to employees is to be changed to owners so that it refers to owners and directors rather than directors and employees.

9. References to domestic violence within the context of claimants living in temporary accommodation are to be changed to include fear of violence in the home or by a former partner.

10. We will make a change to ensure that dual rental liability while adaptations are taking place applies only where a member of the Benefit Unit is disabled and not where the adaptation is to meet the needs of an ineligible person.

11. An additional condition is to be added that, in the case of joint tenants, a non-dependant can only be a non-dependant of one of the joint tenants.

12. Clarification to be made to ensure that no amount of housing cost contribution made by non-dependants can be taken from the mortgage part of the housing element in shared ownership cases

13. Clarification to ensure that in the case of couples, only one person needs to satisfy the exemption criteria from the Housing Cost Contribution, not both.

14. On limited capability for work (LCW), the Main Scheme Regulations will be clarified around how we will require a claimant who is sick and in receipt of a fit-note to digitally confirm their continuing sickness and details of the fit note at least once per assessment period and can provide on demand a statement given by a doctor in accordance with the rules set out in Part 1 of Schedule 1 to the Social Security (Medical Evidence) Regulations 1976.

15. On the treatment of income and capital, and as a further simplification measure, we wish to legislate so that cash received in lieu of concessionary coal will not be treated as an income to be taken into account in calculating an award of Universal Credit.

16. Our general principle is also that a person who has deprived themselves of capital for the purposes of obtaining Universal Credit (or to an increased amount of Universal Credit) should be treated as possessing that capital. We have considered the best way of calculating the amount of capital available and, in particular, allow for a reasonable amount of capital to be eroded over time. So, where a person is treated as possessing capital in this way, we propose to reduce the amount of capital they are considered to possess over time by the amount of Universal Credit to which they would have been entitled were it not for the treatment of the notional capital.

17. On self-employment, we need to ensure that we only disregard business assets that are needed for the company to continue to function. The current draft of Schedule 9 and regulation 48 need tightening a little so that claimants cannot move money into business accounts instead of their personal bank account, for example, in order to gain more UC. We want to be able to take this money into account for UC purposes so that individuals cannot manipulate the amount of state support they receive.

List of respondents

The Committee's thanks and gratitude go to the following individuals and organisations for their submissions to this consultation exercise:

Organisations

1625 Independent People
Addiction Recovery Agency
Advice NI
Affinity Sutton
Age UK
Alliance Homes
Amber Housing
Anchor
Ashiana Network
Asian Women's Resource Centre
Association of British Insurers
Association of Chartered Accountants
Asra Housing Group
Association of Directors of Adult Social Services
Association of Directors of Children Services
Association of Disabled Professionals
Barnardo's
Bexley Women's Aid
Bid and Tender Solutions
Birmingham City Council
Birmingham Crisis Centre
Blue Triangle (Glasgow) Housing Association
Bolton at Home
Bolton Young Persons Housing Scheme
Brighton and Hove Domestic Violence Forum
Bristol City Council
British Property Federation
Bury Council
Butterfly Foundation
Cairn Housing Association
Calan DVS
Carers UK
Centre for Economic and Social Inclusion
Centre for Social Justice
Centrepoint
Cestria Community Housing
Charter Housing Association
Chartered Institute of Taxation
Chartered Institute of Housing
Chartered Institute of Public Finance and Accountancy

Cheltenham Borough Council
Cheshire East Council
Child Poverty Action Group
Children's Society
Citizen's Advice Bureau
Citizen's Advice Bureau, Barnet
Citizen's Advice Bureau, Chelmsford
Citizen's Advice Bureau, Kingston
Citizen's Advice Bureau, Plymouth
Citizen's Advice Bureau, Shropshire
Citizen's Advice Bureau, Stockton
Citizen's Advice Northern Ireland
Colchester and Tendring Women's Refuge
Community Housing Cymru Group
Community Links
Consumer Focus
Contact a Family and Every Disabled Child Matters
Council of Mortgage Lenders
Crisis
Cyrenians
Cumbria Housing Project
Curo Group
Dale's Haven
Day Programme
Deafblind UK
Devon and Cornwall Housing Trust
Dimensions UK
Disability Rights UK
Disabled People Against Cuts
Domestic Abuse Safety Unit
Domestic Violence Support Services W.L.
Dorset Probation Trust
Durham County Council
Durham Police Authority
Durham Women's Refuge
East Durham Homes
East Lancashire Women's Refuge Association
Eastlands Homes
Eaves
Equinox
Ernst and Young LLP

Essex Independent Domestic Violence Advisor Service

Faces in Focus

Family Carer Support Services

Fareham and Gosport Family Aid

Fernbank Care in the Community

First Choice Homes Oldham Limited

Gingerbread

Glasgow Housing Association

Grandparents Plus

Great Places Housing Group

Halton Housing Trust

Hanover Housing Association

Harlow Council

Harlow Education Consortium

Haven, Wolverhampton

Health Energy Advice Team/Liverpool Domestic Abuse Team

Helena Partnerships

Hertfordshire County Council

Hertfordshire County Council Money Advice Unit

Hft

HLG

Homeless Link

Home Saver

HomeStart Epping Forest

Housing for Women

Housing Support Enabling Unit

Housing Systems Limited

Imkaan

Incommunities Group Limited

Independent Choices

Institute of Chartered Accountants in England and Wales

Institute of Chartered Accountants in Scotland

Institute of Revenues Rating and Evaluation

Iranian and Kurdish Women's Rights Organisation

Island Women's Refuge

Islington Carers Centre

Jewish Women's Aid

Kingston Domestic and Sexual Violence Forum

Kirklees Asian Black Women's Welfare Association

Knightstone Housing Association

Knowsley Domestic Violence Support Services

Latin American Women's Rights Service

Law Centre (NI)

Leeds City Council

Liberata

Link Housing Association Limited

Linking Bridges

Liverpool Housing Trust

Liverpool Community Safety and Cohesion Service

Lloyds Banking Group

London Borough of Camden

London Borough of Hackney

London Borough of Merton

London Borough of Newham

Local Government Association

London and Quadrant

London Councils

Look Ahead Housing and Care

Loughton Family Centre

Low Incomes Tax Reform Group

Manchester City Council

Medway Cyrenians

Middlesbrough Council

Midland Heart Limited

miEnterprise Group

Moat

Mosscare

Motor Neurone Disease Association

National Association for the Care and Resettlement of Offenders (NACRO)

National Association of Student Money Advisers

National Association of Welfare Rights Advisers

National Deaf Children's Society

National Farmers' Union

National Association of ALMOs

National Housing Federation

National Institute of Adult Continuing Education, England and Wales

National Landlords Association Limited

National Union of Journalists

National Union of Students

New Charter Housing Trust Group

Newcastle City Council

NHS, North Essex

North Devon Against Domestic Abuse

North West Care and Support Provider Forum

North West Housing Services

North West Landlords' Association

North West Supported Lodgings Forum

One Parent Families Scotland

Orbit Group

Oxfam GB

Papworth Trust

Paypoint

Pennine Domestic Violence Group

Personal Finance Research Centre
Pierhead Housing Association Limited
Plymouth City Council
Poole Probation Centre
Portsmouth City Council
Prince's Initiative for Mature Enterprise
Prince's Trust
Pushing Change
Reach the Charity
Refuge
Regenda Limited
Renfrewshire Council
Residential Landlords Association
Rethink Mental Illness
RISE UK
Riverside Group
Rochdale Boroughwide Housing Limited
Royal Agricultural Benevolent Institution
Royal National Institute of Blind People
Safer Places
Salvation Army
Save the Children
Scottish Council for Single Homeless
Scottish Council for Voluntary Organisations
Scottish Federation of Housing Associations
Scottish Government
Sense Scotland
SHAP Limited
Shelter
Sitra
Social Market Foundation
Society of St James
Solace Women's Aid
South Tyneside Council
South West London and St George's Mental Health NHS Trust
Southampton City Council
St Mungo's
Staffordshire County Council
Staffordshire Supported Housing Network
Standing Together
Stockport Homes
Stop Abuse for Everyone
Supported Housing in Partnership
Surrey Welfare Rights Unit
Surviving Economic Abuse

Sussex Central YMCA
Symphony Housing Group
Tax Aid
Three Rivers Housing Association
Trades Union Congress
Trafford Housing Trust
Transform Housing and Support
Trinity Property
Unison, Northern Region
United Response
Welsh Government
Welwyn Hatfield Women's Refuge
West Kent Housing Association
Westminster Drug Project
White Ribbon Campaign UK
Women's Aid
Women's Aid (Birmingham and Solihull)
Women's Aid (Blackburn)
Women's Aid (Cambridge)
Women's Aid (Chelmsford)
Women's Aid (Leeway)
Women's Aid (Manchester)
Women's Aid (Milton Keynes)
Women's Aid (North Denbighshire)
Women's Aid (North Lincolnshire)
Women's Aid (Port Talbot and Afan)
Women's Aid (Ross-shire)
Women's Aid (Scottish)
Women's Aid (Surrey) (yourSanctuary)
Women's Aid (Sutton)
Women's Aid (Swansea)
Women's Aid (Thurrock)
Women's Aid (Welsh)
Women's Aid (West Mercia)
Women's Aid (West Lothian)
Women's Aid (Wirral)
Women's Budget Group
Women's Resource Centre
YMCA England
YMCA (Central Sussex)
You Trust
Your Homes Newcastle
Zacchaeus 2000 Trust
Zetetick Housing

Individuals

Anderson, Debbie
Banos Smith, Maria
Bartlett, Sophie
Basham, Jane
Bastin, Robert
Bedford, Jill
Beecham, Lord
Bennett, Sarah
Bliss, Joan
Braby, Brian and Janet
Brake MP, Tom
Brand, Lisa
Brittain, Edward
Buchanan, Alison
Bulman, A
Burt, Maxine
Byrne, Helen
Challis, Sue
Chivas, Lixi
Colley, Dan
Collin, David
Cook, Hazel
Cornwell, Lorraine
Cowell, Victoria
Dawson, Kim
Deering, J
Eldridge, Daryon
Ewing, Deborah
Fitch, G
Ford, Elaine
Funnell, Andree
Gellatly, Margaret
Gillespie, Maureen
Goddard, Barry
Graham, Christine
Graham, Robert
Green, Sarah
Grimbleby, Helen
Hartfree, Yvette
Henegan, Blake
Hines, Matthew
Hulcoop, Councillor Maggie
Hoyle, Philip
Hovvels, Councillor Lucy
Humphries, Kate
Hunter, Val
Iainson, Peter
Jarrett, Sharon

Johnston, Councillor Sara
Jones, Gwyneth
Katangodage, Deepika
Keevil, Claire
Kerawala, Dr Firoze
Khan, Ali
La Espuelita, Sandra
Laffar, Jo
Lanaway, Hannah
Lankester, Karen
Lannon, Cara
Lawrence, Barbara
Leggett, Pauline
Lewis, Eileen
Madzikanga, Maxwell
Martin, Graham
McClemont, Emily
McGann, Edward
McTaggart. Richard
Mendolia, Tina
Menzies, J
Miles, A
Mister, Brian
Morgan, Dr Karen
Morrissey, Denise
Morter, Tracy
Necchi-Gheri, Laura
Neuberger, Jeremy
O'Brien, Dr Charlotte
Palmer, Jill
Perry, Douglas
Prosser, Bethan
Pym, Mark
Ramshaw, Maryann
Richens, Rebecca
Roberts, Mike
Roberts, Dr Simon
Robertson, Pamela
Scanlan, Clare
Scott, Judy
Seddon, Brian
Self, Helen
Silver, Gary
Simmons, Dawn
Simmons, Michael
Singer, Sally
Spicker, Professor Paul
Stevenson, Victoria

Szabo, Margaret
Taylor, Caroline
Taylor, Helen
Tean, Jaki
Thorne, Rachel
Toft, Christine
Towersley, Alison
Vine, Malcolm
Waddingham, Lee
Ward, Sam
Watson, Councillor Richard
Weinstock, Pete
White, Lee
Whitehouse, Janet
Wiggins, Sarah
Williams, Dr Peter
Wilcox, Professor Steve
Wright, Kathleen Marcella
Zolobajluk, Maggie